MOVE THAT MOUNTAIN!

By Jim Bakker
with Robert Paul Lamb

Logos International
Plainfield, New Jersey

First Edition, July 4, 1976

MOVE THAT MOUNTAIN!

Copyright © 1976 by Logos International

All Rights Reserved

Printed in the United States of America

Logos International, Plainfield, New Jersey 07060

International Standard Book Number: 0-88270-164-9

Library of Congress Catalog Card Number: 76-10532

"For I assure you,
whoever says to this mountain,
'Be taken up and thrown into the sea,'
and entertains no inner doubt but believes
that what he says will happen,
it shall be so for him."
Mark 11:23

Foreword

Dear Jim,

Many who have moved in the crowded cities of the world have wondered how the gospel could be given to a world whose churches held only one per cent of the world population.

Today as men witness your television ministry bringing the message of Christ to millions at home and abroad, they realize that the Great Commission can indeed be fulfilled through such channels.

In traveling from country to country I hear ministers of various denominations expressing appreciation for the tremendous part you are playing in the evangelization of our world.

Last week in London the convention speaker said concerning yourself, "Seldom have I seen a man with such courage and compassion."

Your life, Jim, has been an amazing drama of trials and triumphs. Your book will be an inspiration to everyone who reads it.

Sincerely,
Willard Cantelon

Dedication

To my mother and father who gave me a Christian heritage without which there would have been no guiding influence in my life;

To my late Grandma Irwin who believed in me and was always a shining example of what a Christian should be;

To William J. Harrison who brought about a turning point in my education by reaching out to a shy young boy;

To my wife Tammy who has been with me on the mountain top and in the valley and who makes me feel that with God's help I can do anything;

To the late Fern Olson who taught me that winning souls was more important than ever being a great preacher;

To Aubrey Sarah who saw "something" in two young people just twenty-one and eighteen years of age and gave us our first revival;

To Pat Robertson who gave me an opportunity to learn all I know today about Christian television and allowed me the freedom to develop a television ministry;

And to all the people I call my "partners" who have made it possible to minister the gospel to this generation . . . for without them there would be no PTL Television Network.

CONTENTS

1

"Oh God, Let me Die!"

Clank! Clank! Clank!

The wind had wrapped several lengths of chain around the grammar school's swing set and with each gust came more clanking as metal slapped against metal.

"Jim Bakker, you can't stay out here much longer."

It was my sister Donna's voice. She was five years older than I and today, the first day of school, it was her job to enroll me in the first grade.

Nervously, I dug my heels into the dirt. "But Donna, I don't feel good today," I fibbed. "Why don't we go back home?"

Donna shook her head. "The bell's gonna ring in a few minutes," she answered, "and when it does we're going into the building."

We had sat for a long time in the safety of the old metal swings. They were spotted alternately with rust and dark green paint. Temporarily, they had become my haven. But their clanking now seemed to heighten my dread of what awaited me inside the dark-looking school building.

1

Move That Mountain

Fear had constantly pervaded my life—from the first time I saw the big "eye" in church. It was a black and white picture of a human eye standing about three feet high on the wall of our Sunday school classroom and, to me, that eye was God Himself. And He was looking directly at me.

When we sang "His eye is watching you, you, you," it only reinforced my misconception. Other songs scared me too, like, "Be careful little feet where you go, be careful little eyes what you see, be careful little tongues what you say. . . ." The big "eye" was always looking and He would get you if you were bad.

Not only was I afraid of God, even my own shadow alarmed me on occasion.

But I felt safe with Donna. She was my close friend and as her little brother she tended to "mother" me.

Rrrrriiiinnnngggg!

"That's the bell," she exclaimed, rushing me toward the school's main entrance. I was inside the busy school building and enrolled with a horde of other kids before I had much time to think about being scared.

But it wasn't long before I did.

I never performed well in grammar school. Teachers told my parents I was a "slow learner." And year after year, my marks were barely good enough to get me to the next grade.

Spelling was my worst subject even though daddy spent many nights grilling me on it. I was such a poor speller that other kids didn't even want me on their spelling team.

My father's name was Raleigh Bakker. He worked as a machinist in a piston ring plant and made a decent living. But I thought we lived in poverty. At Christmas, instead of getting an abundance of toys like most kids, the Bakkers'—two older brothers, Bob and Norman, besides my only sister Donna—got clothes and maybe one or two toys.

I was even embarrassed about my family's house. A cement block structure on Sanford Street in Muskegon Heights, the house had been painted with what daddy thought would be buff-colored paint. It turned out to be orange!

That house stood out on the block, looking like an over-sized Florida citrus. Whenever someone drove me home from school, I'd ask to be dropped off several blocks away so they wouldn't see the house.

It seemed like anything I had was inferior to what other kids had. Year after year, I wore the same tattered blue baseball jacket with prominent white stitching, until the stitching unraveled completely. From the orange house to my dilapidated jacket to my poor school grades, I became filled with deep-seated feelings of inferiority.

The Bakker family was not given to openly saying "I love you." Many families of Dutch origin are like that. They don't show their emotions outwardly and mother and daddy were from the "old school." I knew they loved me but they just weren't vocal about it.

Having been Christians for many years my parents had a rule for the kids: "As long as you sit at our table, you go to church." That included prayer meetings, revivals, special services and any other time the church doors opened at Central Assembly of God.

My oldest brother, Bob, had long since escaped that routine of going to church, but Norman, Donna and I were stuck with it. There was no choice.

There was one bright spot with Sunday though. During the summertime, right after church, the Bakkers plus Uncle Charlie, Aunt Maude and mother's parents—Grandma and Grandpa Irwin—would picnic at the "Ovals" State Park on Lake Michigan. Grandpa Irwin, known as the "kingfish" because of his wily business enterprises, liked to fish while the rest of us sat around and watched Grandma Irwin prepare some of her mouthwatering delicacies.

The only problems we had on the picnics occurred when Grandpa Bakker came along. Years before he had been responsible for starting Central Assembly as a home prayer meeting. I thought he was something of a religious fanatic since he spent much of his time and money passing out gospel tracts and witnessing to people on the streets. When he came on a picnic, he always prayed so long that the food would get cold!

By the time I had reached the seventh grade I was falling into vices common to many boys my age. I started cutting classes with some of the other guys. Then, I began sneaking around smoking.

But one night daddy came home to announce that the Bakkers would be moving to Muskegon.

"Where?" everybody chorused.

"I've found a place on McLaughlin Street," he answered with a smile, "and I think it's going to work out fine."

I was excited about moving. Not only would I get a room all my own, I would be free forever of the embarrassment of that orange house. I'll have to admit, none of my friends had ever kidded me about the house; I guess I was the main cause of my suffering about it. The usual bugaboo, transferring schools, didn't bother me. Since I was so shy, I actually had very few friends.

Things began to change for me at my new school, Muskegon Junior High. Something inside of me seemed to be saying, "You're going to make it." And for the first time, I knew I could.

My shyness had been a barrier to most of my teachers and they had never bothered with me. Mr. Harrison, the photography instructor, was different. "Listen Jim," he said one day while folding up some papers on his cluttered desk, "I believe you've got the natural instincts to become a good photographer."

I didn't know quite what to say, so I just nodded my head. "Yes sir," I finally mumbled.

4

"Oh God Let me Die!"

"Well, I've got a job for you. It's not much of a job, but if you work at it, I can teach you a lot about photography and you can eventually begin taking pictures for the school newspaper. How about it?"

"Okay," I said anxiously, "but what's the job?"

"Emptying the trash cans in the darkroom and cleaning up."

"Well, you're right about it not being much of a job, but it's a deal anyway."

Mr. Harrison was true to his word. After I swept floors, he would teach me how to develop pictures by mixing up the proper chemicals, how to snap the photographs with just the right exposure, and how to arrange subjects for pictures.

Through Mr. Harrison's encouragement, I began to find something I could do. I really did have an ability. Before long, I was ranked at the top of my class in photography. Not only that, but my other grades began to improve as my attitude changed. Next, I moved into advanced photography and became chief photographer of the school newspaper.

Mr. Harrison was also the journalism teacher and he persuaded me to enroll in that as well. The same thing happened. I found something I could do and zoomed to the top of my class. Going into Muskegon Senior High, I was named editor of the school paper.

In speech class I also found that I enjoyed talking before groups. When I told daddy that I needed a tape recorder for class, he surprisingly paid out several hundred dollars for a reel-to-reel model. Several times a week I carried the heavy tape recorder to school and then back home to work on my diction.

That year the photography club was planning its annual dance. It was being called "The Darkroom Hop." The club asked me to emcee the dance, using my tape recorder to play rock-and-roll music. Once again, I stumbled onto something I could do. The

Darkroom Hop was a great success and word spread quickly around school that Jim Bakker was the disc jockey to have at your club's dance.

Club after club began asking me to handle their dances. And the school also permitted me to handle the annual variety shows. Ultimately, I spent more time on extra-curricular activities than with anything else in school.

In the meantime, my folks had moved to one of the old lumber mansions in Muskegon. Built a hundred years before during a "boom" period in the city's economy, the all-wooden structure was located on Webster Street, a tree-lined boulevard where a number of millionaires had once lived. Over the years, the houses had decreased in value and now were modestly priced.

After a variety show one night, all the kids came over for a party at that house, some four hundred of them. Miss Michigan was there, as well as an act from the popular Steve Allen television show, and a band. I was in the limelight completely—the center of attention.

Most high school kids would sell their souls to be popular and I was no exception. I was obsessed with popularity and would do almost anything to get it.

To everybody else, I might have been the picture of fun and success. But inside, I was the lonely, shy boy with the tattered blue baseball jacket. I was also still afraid. Every night when I'd walk up the stairs to go to bed, I was afraid to go to sleep . . . afraid that the old wooden house would catch fire and burn to the ground.

Almost as a precaution, I'd read one verse each night from the New Testament. It was like a ritual I felt I had to do. One night, as I sat on the edge of the bed, I opened the New Testament to read my nightly verse. My eyes fastened strangely on Romans 6:23 and seven words came right off the page at me, "For the wages of sin is death. . . ."

Death!

The word seemed to slap me in the face. Death! Quickly I

snapped off the light and shut my eyes hoping to block out that word. But even with my eyes closed I could see the word. Death!

That word symbolized my condition. Outwardly I was the school's fun-loving disc jockey and editor of its paper. But inside, I was dead. That night the thought of my own death fastened itself upon me. What would it mean? What did God have to do with it?

Although I had been raised in the church, there was little there for a happy-go-lucky type like myself. Everyone seemed so cold and unfeeling.

To my teenage eyes, the church was dead and I wanted no part of it. God just didn't fit into my plans.

One night, I was disc-jockeying a dance. It was a typical sock hop. The high school gym was dark and we had one of those swirling lights attached to the ceiling. The light sent little swirls of blue, red and green color moving around the room as hundreds of kids danced. The music blared from multiple speakers positioned around the gym as I switched record after record on the turntable.

Without warning, a voice spoke to me, "Jim, what are you doing here? You don't belong here."

I looked around the gym. It had seemed like an audible voice, yet apparently I was the only person in the gym to hear it. The blaring music had temporarily receded while the voice sounded as if its speaker was standing right beside me.

I was frightened.

I slapped a long-playing record on the turntable, quickly found a partner, and walked onto the dance floor. Yet even while I danced, I wondered about the voice. Could it be God? Could the big "eye" still be watching me?

I decided to drown myself in activity, any kind of activity. But I couldn't keep from wondering what all this was working up to.

A few weeks later, I was disc-jockeying another dance in the same gym when I looked up and saw my father standing at the door. He never came inside. He just stood there for a long time. "What is going on?" I said to myself.

Daddy never said a word about his coming to the dance. Neither did my mother. And I never mentioned it. Little did I know that they had already been defending me because of the critical remarks of some church people who thought I shouldn't be disc-jockeying dances.

The one friend I could always count on was Grandma Irwin. The sun always seemed to shine at her house, even though it might be raining outside. She had given me the small New Testament that I read at night and her open love had reached inside my heart.

Grandpa Irwin had died while I was in grammar school and now she lived alone in an old, rambling, two-story house. Many times, when it seemed the world was crashing in on me, I drove over to her house and we talked for hours.

When I got ready to leave, she'd wipe a silver wisp of hair behind her ear saying, "Oh, don't be in such a hurry. Won't you stay longer?"

Her refrigerator was always loaded with tasty things to eat which she was ready to share with anyone, especially someone who was in need. Something good to eat and a kind word seemed to be Grandma Irwin's special way.

She was the one person in my life against whom I can never remember feeling even a twinge of resentment. There was something about the way she lived and loved that made you feel special. It was something that I didn't see in the lives of many folks who called themselves followers of Jesus.

Grandma Irwin must have known I was running from God, but she never said a word about it. Her words were always kind, never condemning.

Already eighteen years old, it seemed like I had been running from God all my life . . . and I was still running scared one wintry Sunday night in 1958.

"Oh God Let me Die!"

Over the years, I had spent so much time in church I had become a professional sermon listener. I knew everything there was to know about preachers. I knew when they changed the tone of their voices to make their "appeal" for the altar calls. And that was generally my cue to leave church. I simply couldn't sit through an altar call. There was something about it that bore heavy on me.

That night the preacher got ready to wind up the service. "Now is the time to accept Christ," he was saying emotionally as I took my overcoat in hand. He was still saying "now, now, now" in an almost chilling voice as I slipped out a side door with a cute blonde named Sandy.

Taking my father's '52 Cadillac, Sandy and I drove downtown "cruising." It was the thing most teenagers did in Muskegon—we cruised and talked. But even as we drove the preacher's words, "now, now, now," echoed through my mind. The Cadillac, a spiffy two-tone blue, had a neat radio with speakers in the front and back and I had the volume up loud.

Some of my favorites were playing—Little Richard, Buddy Holly and the Crickets, Ritchie Valens, Fats Domino. Unlike the dead hymns of the church, it was the kind of music I could really appreciate.

It had been an unusually severe winter in Michigan. The snowbanks were piled ten feet high in some places. As more snow fell, the plows just shoved it higher and higher on the sidewalks. People put flags on their car aerials so when a car reached a street corner you could see the little flag over the top of the snowbanks.

The snow began coming down heavily into the cold, crisp night. Large crystal-like flakes were filling the night air as the Cadillac sped downtown. Inside, Sandy and I were having a big time listening to the radio and talking.

Looking at my watch, I suddenly noticed the time. About nine o'clock. "We'd better start heading back to the church, Sandy."

"Why?"

9

"Church will be over in about thirty minutes and my parents will be looking for me then," I said pointing to a bank clock as we drove past.

"Well, okay," she grinned.

I headed back toward the church driving down Terrace Street. Once I reached the intersection with Irwin Street, I could see the church building with its lights blazing through the snow. Central Assembly sat L-shaped on the property and I swung the heavy Cadillac into the church's driveway.

As I drove in, it seemed as if the car bumped against something like the curb.

I didn't think anything about the bump since one of my favorite songs was playing on the radio—Fats Domino singing "Blueberry Hill"—and the two of us sat enjoying the music. "I found my thrill on Blueberry Hill," the song rolled through the Cadillac's twin speakers.

Suddenly, over the top of the music came a voice. It sounded like John Shamel, the church's Sunday school director.

"Jim," he yelled.

I looked around to see where the sound was coming from when I heard the voice scream again, "Jim."

And then I heard the words that sent panic through me. "Jim, you've just run over somebody!"

I quickly leaped out of the car in time to see Mr. Shamel picking up the battered form of a little boy. He looked to be about three years old. The child's legs hung down. His tiny arms were limp. Both wheels of the heavy Cadillac had completely run over his body crushing his lungs immediately.

I began to cry. *I had killed a child.* The life went out of me.

"Oh God," I cried, "Oh God, I didn't want to hurt anybody. Oh God, let me die!"

People started emerging from the church and a crowd gathered quickly. Before I knew it, a police car had arrived and raced off with the little boy for what I thought would be a futile trip to the hospital.

I wandered away from the noise and clamor . . . walking to the side of the church building where I began pounding my fists on the bricks until they bled. Looking up into the still falling snow I pled, "God, help me—help me."

My father found me there and tried to calm me. An eternity passed standing outside in the snow. People walked around talking in muffled voices but they seemed like robots to me. The whole scene was like a bad dream that I couldn't wake up from.

Another police car eventually drove up and I had to sit in the back answering questions. Fortunately, someone had seen the accident. They reported that the little boy had been playing on the snowbank and had slid down into the path of the car.

"What am I going to tell his parents?" I repeatedly asked my father. My mind raced. Would I be charged with manslaughter? Or something even worse? Would I have to go to jail?

Later that night, I went to the hospital with daddy. Sitting in the emergency room among the usual bruised and bleeding, we waited . . . and waited . . . and waited. I thought, any minute somebody will walk in and say the little boy's dead.

To me, the little boy was already dead. And so was I. The fun-loving Jim Bakker, the life-of-the-party, the boy who craved the spotlight was dead.

My world had crashed on me just as I feared it would. For the first time in my life, I surrendered to God. He was my only hope now.

2

My Little Holiness Girl

Unknown to me that cold, snowy night, the same people at Central Assembly who had been praying for me earlier went back into the church and began praying for Jimmy Summerfield, the little boy I had struck. They were asking God for an outright miracle of healing.

I had known the Summerfield family for several years. They had long been members of the church.

While I was sitting in the police car that night with the officers, I had overheard Mr. Summerfield talking. "I feel sorrier for Jim Bakker," he said, "than I do for my own son."

I couldn't believe he and his wife weren't bitter over the situation. But even that night at the hospital, he walked over and shook my hand. "Don't worry about little Jimmy," he said. "He's going to be fine. God will take care of him."

But I wasn't so sure. After several tense hours waiting in the emergency room, my father and I left the hospital without knowing Jimmy's fate. Once home and in bed, I tossed and turned all night—not knowing what to believe or what God would do.

The sun was shining the next day when I awoke and I could hear mother's muffled voice as she spoke into the phone downstairs. I couldn't understand what she was saying, until I heard her say loudly, "Oh, my God. Praise the Lord!"

I heard the phone hit its cradle with a smack and I tensed as her footsteps neared my room. Mother tapped lightly on the door. "Jim, are you awake?" she asked softly.

"Yes, mother," I answered, trying to steady myself for whatever news she was bringing. "Come on in."

Her face was wreathed in smiles when she opened the door. Sitting on the edge of the bed she took my hand and patted it lightly. "Jim," she said with tears beginning to trickle down her face, "God has intervened."

"But how? How did He do it? I thought the little boy was dead!"

She wiped a fresh tear away from her eye. "Jimmy Summerfield is alive," she said. "He's seriously injured but still alive."

But mother," I said shaking my head, "how?"

She smiled through the tears. "They say that several inches of snow was packed on the ground which lessened the impact of the car's tires when they rolled over Jimmy's body."

It was still hard to believe. "But he looked dead, crushed beneath the wheels." My voice began to break.

"But that's the miracle of it. People went back into the church last night and prayed with faith. And He gave us a miracle."

Tears were now flowing freely from my eyes as I began to realize what God had indeed done. Not only was Jimmy Summerfield going to live, but Jim Bakker had been given a new lease on life.

At that moment Jesus became the only thing in my life. I knew I couldn't control my own destiny anymore . . . my future was entirely in the hands of God. I had walked to many church altars weeping before, but God still hadn't become real in my life—until now.

Making Jesus number one in my life brought me into immediate conflict. For the remainder of my senior year, I decided to quit disc-jockeying the school dances. It was a tough decision, but I made it. Most of my teachers and classmates couldn't understand the change in my life.

"'But I'm a Christian now," I tried to explain.

"So what difference does that make?" asked a teacher who was the advisor of a club for which I had promised to handle an upcoming dance.

"It means I can't do it," I answered.

Shaking her head she tried another approach. "You mean you can't do one more even though you promised us earlier?"

It was subtle temptation—making me feel as if I had broken a promise—but I knew I couldn't accept it. The Lord was in control of my life now and the Jimmy Summerfield experience had taught me not to trifle with God.

I visited little Jimmy in the hospital a few days after the accident to present him with a teddy bear. I wasn't sure what I'd find when I walked into his room on that pediatric ward. He was alive, but how much? What kind of damage had his little body sustained? But the reports of his healing were not exaggerated. He was bruised, to be sure, but there was obviously no permanent outward deformity or internal damage. (He has grown, in fact, into a normal, healthy young man today.) I left the hospital in profound silence, a deeply grateful young man.

Late at night, I continued reading my Bible. Only now it meant much more to me. As I read, one passage repeatedly attracted my attention: "And he commanded us to preach . . ." (Acts 10:42).

I tried ignoring it for a long time. But it seemed every time I opened the Bible, out came that verse, night after night. One night I reached for a different Bible—just to see if the book would open to that verse. Sure enough when I opened the pages out came that verse . . . "And he commanded us to preach."

The verse touched something deep inside of me. "God," I prayed that night, "I don't know what you've got in mind for me, but if you want me to preach the gospel, I will."

And for the next several months, an assurance began to grow within me that God was indeed calling me into the gospel ministry. It was that clear. I hadn't made any plans for college, but the issue of my life's calling was settled, and I began to wait for God to show me the next step.

One Sunday I was dropping off some papers for my father at the church office. Giving the papers to Joyce Gore, the church secretary, I noticed an open scrapbook on her desk. "What's that?" I asked.

She smiled, "It's just some mementos of my college days."

I quickly leafed through the book looking at the pictures. "Hmmm. North Central Bible College. Where's that?"

"In Minneapolis."

Noticing some of the school's brochures in the book, I began thumbing through them. The curriculum appeared to be what I was looking for . . . a good full-gospel Bible school with solid Biblical teaching. "How did you like it?" I questioned Joyce.

"Listen," she said seriously, "if you're planning to go into full-time Christian service, this school is the place for you. It's excellent."

Joyce's enthusiasm impressed me. If she thought North Central had something to offer, perhaps it was a place for me to look into. "Thanks a million, Joyce. I'll begin praying about it. Maybe that's where the Lord is leading me."

When some of my high school buddies found out about my

plans for attending Bible college, I became the butt of countless jokes. "Yeah, I can just see Jim Bakker's church now," one of them quipped. "He'll probably have a full orchestra in it. Man, that'll be some church."

I had to laugh too.

The summer of 1959 I began to feel more definitely that God was leading me to North Central Bible College. I located a job in the camera department of the local Sears store to get up enough money for school.

I wasn't the only person from Central Assembly planning to attend North Central. In fact when September rolled around, several kids from church had decided to enroll, including Kenneth May, Mary Archer, Carl Burgess and my cousin Linda Whitum. We left several days early to have time to find jobs. It took almost a day and a half to get to Minneapolis by train and the trip was the more troublesome for the mountain of luggage everybody had brought along.

Arriving in Minneapolis, somehow we expected officials from the school to be waiting to greet us. Nobody came though. Finally, we decided nobody was coming and hailed a taxi. The driver obviously recognized us as "green" kids from out-of-town and saw a chance to make a few extra bucks, which he promptly did. All of the luggage wouldn't fit in the taxi's trunk and he charged us for every extra piece. In fact, we had so much he had to make another trip back to the train station to transport it all.

In the time since I had committed my life to Christ several months before, I had been seeking the Baptism with the Holy Spirit. Yet, nothing had really happened. I had been frustrated by people at church altars trying to help me receive the Holy Spirit.

"Hold on," one would shout. "No, no," another would chime in, "let go and let God have His way." Sometimes it seemed like a shouting match with people trying to help you.

I tried every position possible to receive the Holy Spirit. I stood up. I kneeled down. I saw someone receive lying down. So I tried that. In fact, I tried every position the human body could possibly maneuver into in receiving the Spirit. Yet for me, the results were the same. Nothing happened.

In the long run, I simply became frustrated.

For several months, I had prayed for the Lord to baptize me with the Holy Spirit before school started. Day after day, I offered that prayer to God. And yet when the night before school was to open arrived I still hadn't received the baptism.

Several friends invited me to a meeting at the nearby Minneapolis Evangelistic Auditorium. Joyce had already told me about the church and I went.

At the close of the service, Russell Olson, the church's pastor, said, "I feel there are several people here tonight who've never received the Holy Spirit. This is your night. God is here to give you what you ask for."

Something inside of me responded. I knew his words were meant for me.

"If you've never received the baptism," he said, "I want you to go to the center of the room and we'll pray for you."

Without even thinking. I walked toward the center of the room with several others. I had sought God so long and so hard without success. "Lord," I said in desperation, "I give up."

The moment I spoke those words, the Lord baptized me with the Holy Spirit and immediately I began speaking in a language I hadn't learned. For what seemed like hours I was lost with God. When I drifted back to earth, the room was practically empty of people and I was singing.

"I've been with Jesus and I'm so happy," I sang, "and I can feel it in my soul!" He had answered my prayer and empowered me to serve Him. I had already read the entire Bible a couple of times. Yet after receiving the baptism, there was a freshness to it far greater than I had ever experienced before. Now it was as if I couldn't get enough of the Bible.

My Little Holiness Girl

I spent all my free time in the school's basement prayer room reading the Bible and praying. I fasted often and was continually seeking God. Sometimes I had to fast because I was without money; other times I fasted as God taught me through His Word.

That first year at North Central, I was known as a "Holy Joe." I had turned my back on the world completely. In fact, I didn't even date that first year. My high school sweetheart and I had drifted apart. And now my life just didn't have time for girls. I simply went to class and stayed in the prayer room.

I began to eat a little more frequently after I got a job cleaning the school's classrooms and restrooms. Near the end of the school year, my meals improved considerably when I landed a job as a busboy in the Fountain Room, a posh restaurant in the Rothchild-Young-Quinlin store.

Lena Williams, the Fountain Room's manager, had worked her way up from a waitress and she knew her job. "There's one thing in this restaurant that's your enemy," she said on my first day of work.

"What's that?"

"Fuzzies," she said sharply, leading me by the hand to a steam table.

She pointed to a piece of lint hanging above the table. "See that? That's a fuzzy and I don't want any of them in this kitchen. Okay?"

"Yes, indeed." I knew it was going to be hard work with Lena in charge, but I couldn't pass by such a good opportunity.

September 1960, I entered my second year at North Central. I continued studying and praying diligently, and working at the Fountain Room. But one day I passed a girl in the school's hallway . . . my neck almost broke as I turned to watch her walk away.

She was absolutely the cutest girl I had ever seen. She was wearing white socks, gym shoes and a stiff purple crinoline skirt

19

and looked to be less than five feet tall. Her long blonde locks fell below her shoulders in a style that looked oddly out of date for such a pretty girl.

Even without makeup, she was a little doll. North Central was small enough that finding out her name wasn't much of a problem.

It was Tammy LaValley and she was from International Falls, Minnesota. There was only one problem. She was engaged and the wedding date had already been set.

And that, it seemed was that.

But still, I'd occasionally see her in the hallways. And she would always wink at me. I thought to myself, "That's not right for an engaged girl to do." Little did I know that that was Tammy's way of being friendly and she was winking at a lot of other people, too.

One day, I noticed she wasn't wearing her engagement ring any more. And in Bible school, the word spread fast. She had broken up with her fiance. It was time to make my move. I was no longer working as one of the school's janitors, but I did have a school job checking the students in and out of their dorm. They were supposed to sign a register when leaving the dorm, and I worked several hours in the evening at the desk in the lobby.

The next night after I noticed Tammy's engagement ring was missing, I spoke to her as she was signing the book on my desk. "Excuse me," I said, "I'm Jim Bakker."

"Yes, I know. I'm Tammy LaValley."

"Uh, Tammy," I nervously cleared my throat, "I'm going over to the ice skating rink Saturday night. Would you be interested in going?"

She shook her head. "I don't think I can, Jim," she said picking up her books and walking up the stairs, "but thanks anyway."

I was devastated.

But later I found out from a mutual friend, Peggy Elliot,

that Tammy thought it was too soon to be going out after having just broken her engagement of several years.

I had found a friend in Peggy and she ended up being a matchmaker. Living on the same third floor of the dormitory as Tammy, they became close friends. She told me that Tammy really liked me and, in turn, told Tammy that I liked her.   .

But the truth was, I was falling madly in love. I was absolutely, totally infatuated with this effervescent eighty-three pound blonde. She didn't wear a touch of makeup, so I nicknamed her "my little holiness girl."

Even though Peggy was continually bringing encouraging reports about how much Tammy liked me, I was distressed because each night Tammy would go ice skating with about five or six guys from the school. Night after night, I watched them parade right by my little desk in the lobby. Being from a large family, Tammy thought nothing of going ice skating with a group of guys. They were all big brothers to her, but I was clearly irked by the situation.

One night on the way back to her room, Tammy reached across my desk and handed me a small bell from her ice skates. It had come off while she skated.

My heart flickered as I thought "finally we're beginning to make some progress here." But a few nights later, Tammy and the parade of guys were back again.

That night when she returned to the dorm I handed the bell back. "No, thanks," I said curtly, trying to show my displeasure with her skating escapades.

"Okay." She sounded disappointed and looked, I hoped, a little crushed.

But Peggy persevered in her self-appointed task, and after several weeks she finally convinced me to ask Tammy out again. This time Tammy said "yes" and on Wednesday night we were walking through the fresh December snow some fifteen blocks away to the Minneapolis Evangelistic Auditorium.

That night I could hardly wait to get out of church for wanting to walk back to school and talk with Tammy. When, at last, the service did end and we were on our way, I impulsively decided to kiss her. Stopping on the sidewalk, I announced, "Tammy, kiss me." She looked at me strangely.

"Well, kiss me," I repeated firmly.

Finally, she reached up on tiptoes and her soft lips melted into mine. She seemed to be in a temporary state of shock. Moments later, we were both in shock when a tall, muscular guy walked up while we were embracing. "What are you doing?" he growled in a deep voice.

Both of us fell back, temporarily frightened. We didn't know what he had in mind, so we ran off together giggling down the street.

I didn't have a ring for Tammy, so the next day I bought an identification bracelet. That night, as we walked to church once again, I decided I would pull a familiar tactic to see if she loved me.

"Tammy," I said as we walked back toward school after the service, "I don't think I can date you anymore."

"But . . . why?"

"Well, I'm falling in love with you and I've got to finish Bible school."

"I am too," Jim.

"You are?"

"Yes!" she exclaimed.

I took off the ID bracelet. "In that case, I want you to wear this."

A tear slipped slowly down her face. "Jim, what does this mean?"

"I want to marry you."

She nodded her head. "This is so quick, but I want to marry you, too."

The grapevine quickly got the word around school that we were engaged. Nobody could really believe it. In fact, there were times I could hardly believe it. Everything seemed to move so rapidly.

My parents couldn't believe it either. During a break in classes in February, Tammy came home with me. She and my sister Donna became friends quickly. They spent many hours in Donna's old room chatting and Tammy repeatedly tried on the gown Donna had worn at her wedding.

I spent my time talking with mother and daddy. "I'd rather you wait to get married, Jim," my father said over a cup of coffee, "until after you finish Bible school."

"But daddy. . . ."

Mother spoke up. "Jim, it's not that we have anything against Tammy. It's just we think you ought to wait."

It seemed like I was beating my head against a brick wall trying to convince them. They were firm but friendly about the subject . . . but they just wouldn't hear of me getting married now. In fact, we had already loaded Donna's wedding gown in the car when my father retrieved it and brought it into the house.

But Tammy and I were deeply in love. She was the only girl for me. I believed God had brought us together and we were destined to be married. And for the next several months, we saw each other almost daily. In the afternoons and weekends, we went ice skating, and at nights and on Sundays, we went to church.

Ultimately, our close relationship began affecting our studies. Both of us realized it was either get married or break up.

Tammy loaned me fifty dollars as the down payment for her ring and one night, while services were under way at church, I slipped the diamond on her finger. We were sitting on the church platform and Tammy gasped loudly. Several people looked our way and Tammy blushed brightly through her tears.

We set the wedding date for April 1, 1961.

Russell Olson, pastor of Minneapolis Evangelistic Auditorium, married us in the church's "Garden of Prayer." The place had been a wine cellar at one time and was the same room in which I had received the baptism.

That day we both worked at our regular jobs. I was still a busboy at the restaurant and Tammy was a sales clerk at F.W. Woolworth's. Together we probably brought home a grand total of eighty dollars a week. I had sunk so much money in Tammy's engagement ring I couldn't afford an expensive wedding band—and since she'd loaned me the down payment she didn't have any extra money either. We had to settle for wedding rings from Woolworth's. Unfortunately, they continually turned green on our fingers and we went through about twenty rings before we were able to afford some that didn't tarnish.

Tammy was going to wear a red dress trimmed in black but Lena Williams ruled that out. Instead she wore a pale green dress and Lena provided some white gloves. Following the youth service, which I led that night, Tammy and I were married. Bob Silke, my roommate, was the best man and my sister Donna, who was now living in Minneapolis, served as matron of honor.

Pictures of the event were lost forever when Pastor Olson's camera wouldn't work—but Tammy and I were deliriously happy and, most importantly, in love.

Our finances wouldn't allow a honeymoon trip, so we simply went to the third floor walk-up apartment Lena Williams had helped us get. Lena, in spite of her strict ways at work, had taken me under her wing and practically "mothered" me. Through her help, we were able to get a sixty-dollar-a-month apartment right next door to her. Some college guys had had the place before and Playboy nudes decorated most every wall in the place. But Tammy and I quickly removed them.

The bathroom had been painted a shocking red, including the ceiling. So we repainted it in Tammy's favorite color, soft lavender, trimmed in white. Tammy even made ruffled curtains to go around the base of the huge antique tub which stood on massive animal-like legs.

Next, we did the kitchen in pink and black. Later we rescued a usable couch from the nearby Salvation Army store and filled the apartment with scatter rugs from Woolworth's. As simple as the place was, it was a little bit of heaven for the newly-married Bakkers.

Financially, the times were rough. We frequently went out to retrieve deposits on our Coke bottles to get enough money for bread and some sandwich spread until payday rolled around. Other times, we took a can of tomato soup heated in the popcorn popper and made a meal out of it.

Lena tried to help out as often as possible. She gave us cracked china and bent silverware from the Fountain Room. But her prize gift was a pink floral print that we proudly hung over our living room couch.

A few weeks after we were married, I found Tammy behind the kitchen door crying. At first, I thought she was unhappy over our tight finances.

But after it happened a time or two, I finally asked, "What in the world is the matter, honey?"

"Jim, my folks have never met you."

I cradled her face in my hands. "That's no problem. We'll take off some time and pay them a visit."

I didn't know that was only part of Tammy's problem. I had always thought she was an only child, especially since she always looked so well-groomed. But, in fact, Tammy had seven brothers and sisters, and she was worried at what I would think. She didn't tell me about her fears until much later, so I was surprised to find such a large family when we arrived in International Falls, nestled on the Canadian border.

Even more surprising was a quaint feature of her parent's old two-story house. It had an outdoor toilet! And in International Falls, where it can reach forty below zero in the winter—an outdoor toilet can be quite an adventure.

So, for that matter, was taking a bath. Tammy brought in two large galvanized tubs filled with steaming water. I just looked at them.

"What do I do with them?" I scratched my head.

"Silly," she laughed, "you bathe in them."

I had never had any experience with such things having been accustomed to the worldly luxuries of a bathtub. So I promptly sat my bottom down in one tub and my feet in the other and started bathing.

Tammy laughed so hard that tears streamed down her face. "No," she howled, "you sponge off. You don't get in the tub. You wash with one tub of water and rinse with the other."

And that's the way the first visit to Tammy's house went. It was absolutely wild. In fact, they even had a silly game where you placed your tongue on the frost-covered doorknobs of the house. The only problem occurred if someone opened the door.

Practically everyone in the family either played a musical instrument or sang . . . so, while her mother turned out mounds of delicious fudge from the kitchen, everybody else gathered around the piano playing and singing. Even Tammy's Grandma Fairchild, who brought back fond memories of my Grandma Irwin, joined in the singing.

It was the kind of zany environment in which nobody could stay a stranger for long.

3

"I'm Quitting the Ministry"

Since Tammy and I knew it was against North Central's rules to marry while attending school, we didn't bother going back to class. A few weeks after the wedding, a letter arrived from school officially advising us that we were no longer students at North Central Bible College.

In addition to our full-time jobs, we became youth leaders at Minneapolis Evangelistic Auditorium. Russell Olson and his wife, Fern, were co-pastors of the church.

Fern Olson was, and is, a gifted preacher. I was thrilled to get her as a Sunday School teacher. Sunday after Sunday, she instructed us in the deep things of God—particularly faith—and I tried to absorb everything she said. Little did I realize how vital it would be to me in coming years.

"What's the key to success as an evangelist?" I asked her one Sunday morning after the class lesson had ended.

Without a moment's hesitation, she said, "Results."

I nodded my head recognizing the truth of what she said.

"If you want to be a successful evangelist and have

27

churches call you," she continued, "you must get results. It's nice to have a theory, but only results will demonstrate the value of the theory."

Russell Olson was, and is, a talented Bible teacher and dynamic soul-winner. The Olsons, together with the anointed teachers and evangelists who constantly ministered at the church, provided a rich Bible school for Tammy and me.

The next several months at the church proved to be some of the most valuable in our lives. Not only were we being taught the great lessons of the Bible, but as youth leaders we were able to put these same lessons right back into practice.

Faith—simple childlike trust in God—was one of the cornerstones of the Olsons' ministry. They challenged us continually to believe God as Abraham had who "staggered not at the promise of God through unbelief; but was strong in faith, giving glory to God; and being fully persuaded that, what he [God] had promised, he was able also to perform" (Romans 4:20, 21).

One Sunday morning in church, I felt God urging me to empty my wallet into the collection plate. I knew I had twenty-five dollars. "But that's for bills and groceries" I objected in my mind. I relented at last, and when the offering plate came, I put the whole twenty-five in. Almost immediately I began praying, "Lord, have somebody ask us out to dinner today. And Lord, please remember, You'll have to take care of our groceries for a week, too."

Two hours later the service ended and we headed for an exit. "Jim," a voice sounded behind me, "how are you?"

I looked around into the face of one of the church's elders. "Fine," I said, "just fine." Yet, inside, I was worried that I had no money for groceries.

The elderly man shook my hand and in so doing gave me two ten dollar bills! "Praise the Lord," I said to myself.

Tammy had momentarily disappeared in the crowd, but I soon found her near the exit. "Honey, look what I've got," she announced holding up a five dollar bill.

"That's beautiful," I said, "and I was just given twenty dollars."

Down the building's steps toward the main street, several classmates from North Central were standing at the side door. "Say, what are you doing for lunch," Jim Drown asked us.

"Nothing really," I answered.

"Well, come on with us," he said, "I'll treat you."

Tammy and I exchanged glances while we praised the Lord inwardly for his goodness. Once we got back to the apartment, the folks who'd taken us to lunch gave us enough money for two weeks' groceries. We had trusted God in a little thing and he had blessed us in an even larger way.

Not only did the Olson's teach basic faith as the only way to walk with God, but they also were expert teachers of Romans 8:28: "And we know that all things work together for good to them that love God, to them who are the called according to his purpose." It was a lesson I would need to remember many times.

During the early fall, Dr. Samuel Coldstone came to the church telling a marvelous story of his evangelistic endeavors in South America. Dr. Coldstone was planning to use a fancy yacht once owned by Hollywood actor Errol Flynn to sail up and down the Amazon River. His idea was to reach the thousands of people living along the banks of the river.

At the time, Tammy and I had been crying out to God for His leading in our lives. We just didn't know what direction to take. Then along came Dr. Coldstone and his plans for the Amazon.

Right away we were excited about the plans for the work and Dr. Coldstone agreed that we might accompany him on the condition that we must raise our own support money. Not only were we impressed with Dr. Coldstone's plans, but many others in the church were as well, and he collected thousands of dollars for his South American ministry.

29

Several weeks later I was at the altar praying with Tammy following the close of a service, when one of the church's elders walked up. "Jim," he said laying his hands on my shoulders, "I believe I have a word from the Lord for you. You are going to have two important decisions to make in the next several weeks. For the first decision your answer is to be no. For the second decision your answer is to be yes. The Lord also wants you to get plenty of rest. If you don't, the devil will use it against you. God has called you and Tammy together as a team. Your work for Him will bear much fruit as you go united."

Tammy and I sensed the authenticity of those brief words and that night we committed the whole matter to Him in prayer. I had almost forgotten it until the telephone rang several days later. It was my brother, Norman, calling from Chicago.

"Jim," he announced, "I've got an exciting deal for you."

"Really, what is it?"

"I've got a great location for a new restaurant, and I want you to come to Chicago to work with me."

"Norman, you can't be serious. I don't have any experience in the restaurant business, except as a busboy. Besides I've got a few bills I need to pay off."

"Listen, don't worry about anything," he urged grandly. "If you come to Chicago for me, I'll pay off all your debts."

"Well, I don't know," I said finally.

Realizing I wasn't sure about the matter, Norman promised to call back the next day. The minute I hung up, I remembered the prophecy at church. Tammy had been listening to the whole conversation and she quickly spoke up. "Honey, I think this is where we're supposed to say no."

True to his word, Norman called back the next day and I told him I couldn't come to Chicago. Once I had obeyed what I believed was a genuine word from the Lord, I felt greatly relieved in my heart, even though I didn't know how we'd pay off our bills or raise the money to go with Dr. Coldstone.

I was still in doubt about the matter when Pastor Aubrey Sarah from Burlington, North Carolina came to our church to hold a revival. Pastor Sarah had an unusual ability with words. As an artist paints pictures with various colors, Pastor Sarah painted pictures with his words. He brought forth some of the most vivid descriptions of Jesus I had ever heard.

Pastor Sarah took an immediate liking to Tammy and me. When he heard about our plans to raise money for a missionary trip, he suggested that we come down to his church and preach a revival there.

"You mean in North Carolina?" Tammy and I said almost in unison.

"Yes," he laughed. "That would be a perfect way to get some experience and earn some money for the trip."

"Sounds great to us," I agreed and quickly made arrangements.

Right after that, Tammy and I took a small tour of various churches in Minnesota and Michigan explaining our plans for South America. Before the trip was over, not only had we raised our support, but I also had all the sermons God wanted me to preach in Burlington.

After selling some of our furniture and giving away the rest, we paid off our few bills and had just enough money to take the bus from Minneapolis to Burlington. Pastor Olson, however, heard about my plans and nipped them in the bud. "Jim," he said seriously, "you can't possibly do that. You'll be so tired when you get there you won't be able to preach."

"What'll I do?"

"I think the Lord can take care of this," and he reached into his pocket to produce enough money for us to fly first class to North Carolina.

Move That Mountain

Pastor Sarah greeted us warmly at the airport. On the way to the church, we stopped off to eat before the services. The gum-chewing waitress asked for our orders. "Hamburgers," Tammy and I answered.

"You want it all-the-way?" she asked, her pencil raised high over her order pad.

I looked at Tammy puzzled. I had never heard that expression before. "What does 'all-the-way' mean?" I asked.

"That means with slaw," she giggled as if any idiot knew what "all-the-way" meant.

Not only were we introduced to hamburgers "all-the-way," but we also discovered hush puppies, grits, Carolina red clay and warm southern hospitality. Since neither of us had ever traveled much out of our home states, it was a real education. So was my first attempt at preaching.

That night when I got up to preach I was unusually nervous. Here was the culmination of everything since I had been saved . . . my training in church . . . the teaching in Bible school . . . the practical work in Minneapolis. It all had brought me to this one moment when I would get up and preach the gospel just as the Lord called me to do.

Being a little unsure of what exactly would happen when I got into the pulpit, I brought along a handful of notes just in case I ran out of things to say. I figured I would preach my heart out, give an altar call and step back for the results. After all that's the way Billy Graham did it, and I was sure to set the woods on fire once I could develop my style. I was out to evangelize the world.

And I preached my heart out, gave the altar call . . . and nothing happened.

I couldn't believe it! My plan had seemed so simple. But instead of people streaming forward to the altar, the congregation just sat back staring at me. Some of the people even looked as if they were glaring.

After the service, I walked back to Pastor Sarah's office

32

feeling like the end of the world had come. I got down on my knees and sobbed my heart out into the green carpet. I didn't know, but Tammy had been standing behind me several minutes. Her voice brought me back to reality, "What's the matter, Jim?"

"I'll never preach again." My heart was shattered. The results Fern Olson spoke about had not come—I was a failure.

I was too dejected to talk with Tammy. She left the room for a few minutes and came back with Pastor Sarah.

"Brother Sarah, I'm finished. I'm quitting the ministry." He looked at me with a faint smile on his face and shook his head. He could see how much I was feeling sorry for myself.

"Listen Jim," he said softly, "I don't care if you preached the world's worst sermon. You've got to leave the results with the Lord."

Tammy came over and knelt down beside me.

"I don't care what your message was like," he said. "When you're finished preaching, you hold your head high and you walk to the front door. You look people straight in the eye and you shake hands with them as they leave the church."

"Then, you don't think I should quit the ministry?"

He laughed. "Certainly not, let's just trust the Lord and see what happens. Okay?"

"Okay," I answered weakly.

Somehow I was convinced that Pastor Sarah was right, and for the next week and a half I did what he suggested. I preached, left the results with God and walked to the back to shake the people's hands.

That gave me new freedom, but the results were essentially the same: nothing.

That is, until the last two nights. I gave my testimony of how Christ had found me. Something began to happen. A cute teenage girl left her seat to come forward for prayer. Several rows back, her boyfriend was still in his seat. He seemed to be looking the situation over. Obviously, it was his first time in such a service.

But after a while he joined his girlfriend who shortly thereafter began speaking in tongues and praising God softly. Within a few minutes, the young man raised his hands and began to cry. As the Spirit of God touched him, he began to speak in tongues and roll on the floor. Dressed in a dark blue suit, he picked up every piece of lint on the church's carpet as he rolled from one end of the building to the other while the congregetion began singing and praising God.

Even though Tammy and I had been raised in Pentecòstal churches, we had never seen a genuine "holy roller" before. And of all things, this one turned out to be a staunch Presbyterian.

By the time the meetings ended, a number of people testified that they had been saved and filled with the Holy Spirit, and many said they had been healed of physical afflictions. "See what I mean Jim," Pastor Sarah commented. "You always have to leave the results with God. He's the only one who can change the situation."

Pastor Sarah felt that the revival had been a success and began calling other pastors throughout North Carolina. On his word, they began scheduling us for upcoming meetings.

We would need the revivals. By the time the Burlington meeting had ended, we discovered the true story about Dr. Coldstone. There was no Errol Flynn yacht, nor any ministry in South America. Dr. Coldstone was not to be found anywhere.

Instead of using our money to travel to South America, Tammy and I picked out a white Valiant from a Burlington car lot operated by a man from Pastor Sarah's church. We also wrote a letter to our supporters explaining the situation with Dr. Coldstone, and telling them that now we were going into evangelism in America.

The night before we were to leave Burlington for our next revival, we sat up talking with Pastor Sarah. Tammy and I were still a little disheartened over the Dr. Coldstone matter.

"You know," Pastor Sarah said encouragingly, "I think in

34

time you'll be able to look back on this and see that Dr. Coldstone did you a big favor."

"A big favor?"

"That's right. I think the Lord used him to get you and Tammy out of your nest in Minneapolis and on the road of evangelism. It might look a little hard to believe right now, but in time I think you'll see it. He didn't really do you in. He did you a big favor."

Remembering the Olsons' teaching on Romans 8:28, I had to agree with Pastor Sarah. "I guess you're right. If all things work together for good, then this has got to produce good."

4

On the Road for Jesus

Pastor Howard Fortenberry invited us next to preach in Greensboro and, following that, pastors were calling us from all over the state. Gastonia, Wilmington, Newton, High Point—all became familiar stops to us as we moved back and forth across North Carolina.

A few months after I had preached in one small town, word filtered back that we had received an extra large financial gift from the couple with whom Tammy and I had been staying while there. The money was supposed to have been in addition to the church's love gift. I was stunned by the news since it wasn't true and the implication was that Tammy and I had taken advantage of this elderly couple.

I didn't really know what to do about the situation, so the next time I was in Greensboro I sought advice from Pastor Fortenberry who was also district presbyter.

"Jim, don't make a big thing out of this, but whenever you're in that area again, go see that pastor and tell him what you heard."

I talked it over with Tammy, and we agreed to follow his advice. In a few weeks we were back in that area. Sitting down with the pastor and his wife, I explained that I never received any such extra contribution. "Jim, I believe you," the pastor said earnestly. "It was obviously an unfounded rumor. I'm glad you stopped off to chat with me and we now know the truth."

That established a precedent for Tammy and me. Never again would we stay in the homes of church members while we were leading meetings. We would stay instead with the pastors—and only visit a private home when the pastor accompanied us. As more time passed, we also learned not to cultivate close friendships with any of the church members because of the jealousy that might arise between some pastors and their congregations.

It became a life of traveling from one town to another. Sometimes it was lonely. But Tammy and I were a team and we determined to do our best in whatever circumstances. Because of the constant travel, we became each other's only friend.

At the close of many meetings, the pastor would pump my hand soundly saying, "Here's a token of our deep love and appreciation for you and your fine work."

The token would sometimes amount to no more than thirty dollars for a week's or even two weeks' work. In some cases, it seemed like the harder we worked the smaller the offerings were.

Although it was sometimes difficult to pay our bills because of our scanty income, the Lord primed us to walk in faith and blessed us continually when we did.

About six months later, an invitation came to minister in Anchorage, Alaska. "We have barely enough money to get there," Tammy was disconcerted.

"I know," I answered thinking about the situation. "Why don't we go ahead and make the trip and see what God will do."

"Well, I'm game if you are," she smiled.

Unfortunately, upon our arrival in Alaska, Tammy came

down with a painful kidney infection and had to remain in bed for several days. We were sleeping on canvas cots in the nursery of a church, and Tammy ended up spending all her time inside the building. Unknown to me, she had been praying for the Lord to teach her to play the organ, and while she was staying in the church, she practiced every day until she managed pretty well. When she had recuperated, she joined me in the Anchorage churches as well as at a children's home in Valdese that was later destroyed by an earthquake.

We had hoped to bring back some souvenirs and one day we stopped by a jewelry store. Inside, the store manager called us over. "Who are you folks?" he asked with a smile.

"I'm Jim Bakker," I said shaking his outstretched hand, "and this is my wife, Tammy."

"Well from the sound of your voice I can tell you aren't from around here," he laughed. "Where's home?"

I had to laugh, too. "We're from Michigan and Minnesota," I answered, "but we've come here from North Carolina to preach in various churches."

Calling his wife over, he introduced her. "Isn't this beautiful," she said. "We're Christians, too. I'm so glad the Lord brought you by our shop to visit with us. Why don't you pick out something from our showcase to take back home with you?"

Tammy spoke up abruptly, "Oh no, we couldn't do that."

"Well in that case," the woman said, "let me do it for you." And with that she reached into the showcase and pulled out two beautiful Alaskan black diamond rings.

We were floored at their generosity . . . yet we realized it was simply the Lord's way of fulfilling the desires of our hearts. Not only that, they gave us a large donation and we drove home with more money than we had arrived with.

Some of the lessons in faith came in the strangest ways. For a long time, Tammy had been asking me to buy her a shawl.

Yet our finances just didn't leave room for such a purchase. "Honey," I said repeatedly, "that's one request God will have to answer. We don't have the money for it."

A few weeks later we were holding a meeting in Tarpon Springs, Florida, and it was hot. Even though it was autumn, it seemed as if we were in the midst of a heat wave. I was sitting at the kitchen table preparing my sermon when a knock came on the door.

"I'll get it," Tammy shouted walking to the door.

I heard the door open and a woman's voice, "Tammy, I just wanted you to have this." She handed Tammy a large gift box.

"Thanks ever so much."

"It's a white shawl," the woman said, "and I made it for you. I know it sounds a little strange in this weather, but it seemed the Lord said to do it."

Through that the Lord showed me that He was concerned with the little things, too. My faith was growing in several directions at once.

Tammy's musical talents had always been an important part of our services. Her mother, a natural musician, had taught Tammy as a child to play the piano. Together with her singing, it made an indispensable contribution to our ministry—I preached while she did the music. Yet, Tammy wanted to become more versatile in her music.

One Sunday morning we were standing outside a church chatting with members of the congregation at the close of a meeting. An elderly man walked up to Tammy and shook her hand. "Do you have an accordion?" he asked.

"No, I don't."

He looked at her seriously, "Well, if you had one, would you play it?"

Tammy's eyes popped open wide, "I sure would!"

He walked away momentarily and came back carrying a new Horner accordion complete with a travel case. "This is the best money can buy," he said proudly. "Now play it for the glory of God."

Tammy didn't have any idea how she would learn to play the accordion, but the Lord took care of that, too. The pastor at our next revival was an accomplished accordion player and he willingly taught her. In three weeks, Tammy sounded like a professional with it.

After a couple years on the evangelistic field, we had fallen into a monotonous pattern. Some evangelists get put up at motels, but in our case we continually wound up staying at the preacher's house. Everybody, it seemed, wanted to "mother" us.

One day, we scheduled a meeting with a sizable church and the minister wrote a flowing letter back, "We have a beautiful evangelist's apartment, and we'd love to have you stay there while you're ministering in our church."

The thought of some genuine privacy appealed to us both, and for the next few months we talked continually about what it would be like staying in the "evangelist's apartment." Time passed quickly, and we finally drove up for the meetings.

Hurriedly we got all the normal introductions out of the way with the minister and he said, "You folks must be tired. Let me take you over to the apartment I promised you."

We were all primed and ready. We had waited six months for this.

But as the pastor led us through the church sanctuary and up a long, winding stairway our hearts fell. The church was an old Gothic-style building, the kind in which you could expect to see bats flying about, and the evangelist's apartment was located at the head of the creaky stairs in the rear. The place was dank and musty, a perfect setting for a horror movie.

"The apartment doesn't have a tub or shower," the preacher announced, "but the church's bathroom is on the first floor and you can use that. The only running water is in the church kitchen. So you'll have to bathe in there."

41

"Oh," Tammy tried to sound pleasant while we both moaned inside.

The pastor started for the door, "I'll be back to check on you before the service."

We stood in the center of the room listening to the building groan and creak as the winter wind beat against it. Then, in a moment, the pastor opened the door and popped his head in. "One more thing," he said, "there's an old friend of mine who stays in the apartment when he comes through town. He has a key. If he happens to stop off while you're here, just tell him you're using the apartment and he can't stay here. He's over sixty-five years old and half-deaf, so be sure you speak loudly to him."

I tried to force a smile, "You can be sure I'll speak loudly if he comes in."

The pastor closed the door and we heard his steps going down the stairs. "And you can be sure that guy will hear me if he comes in here while I'm in bed," Tammy announced huffily.

For almost a full week neither of us did much sleeping. We had visions of the old man crawling into bed with us in the middle of the night. And the building made so many weird noises that Tammy was continually asking me, "Jim, what was that?" Then, when we both finally settled down for the night, any movement in the bed would cause the worn slats to fall out and the whole bed would collapse onto the floor. Time and again, we had to put that bed back together.

The church's kitchen windows lacked curtains, so we draped our extra towels over them while taking a sponge bath. It reminded me of my first visit to Tammy's house.

Tammy and I never romanticized about our accommodations after that. We learned to expect nothing. That way we were never disappointed, and we were freer to praise God in whatever circumstances we found ourselves.

But as our second year on the road stretched into three, we began feeling more like vagabonds. Since we had given up our apartment in Minneapolis, we had no home of our own. Vacations were always spent with our parents—so we were constantly living with other people.

The strain was beginning to tell on us and we began praying for a travel trailer.

Travel trailers are expensive and since our earnings varied so radically from place to place, it seemed almost impossible that we could afford one. But God had primed us through the small things like the shawl, the accordion, and the Alaskan black diamonds—we were ready to believe Him for something bigger now!

Back in the mountains of North Carolina, we were doing a week-long revival at an Assembly of God church. Besides the revival, we were also holding additional meetings for the children in the church. As the week progressed, people began giving large amounts of money. It was only a small church, with maybe fifty members, but people were dropping hundred-dollar bills into the offering plate!

Nobody knew that we had asked God for a travel trailer, but by the time services had ended over fifteen hundred dollars had been donated to our ministry. It was a miracle of God's unlimited provision.

Tammy and I were almost embarrassed to go down to the postage stamp-sized bank and get money orders for our bank account back home. Figuring everything, we had enough money for a down payment on a new travel trailer, and we began making plans to pick one up on our next trip to Michigan.

We had decided on a twenty-eight-foot Holiday Rambler with a complete bedroom, bath, kitchen and living room with full-sized furniture. At last, I wouldn't feel like I was robbing some mother's child of its food when I raided the refrigerator late at night. Now, I would have my own refrigerator to raid— compliments of the Lord.

At the dealer's lot in Muskegon, the sparkling new Holiday

Rambler was hitched up to our used 1959 Cadillac and we were off down the road to our next revival.

By late afternoon of the next day, we were within forty miles of our destination in Virginia. We had already slept one night in the trailer and were thrilled with God's provision.

Pulling through a small town and across some railroad tracks, I noticed the car went up in front and down in back. It produced a slight jarring motion.

"Doesn't the car look higher in front?" I asked.

"Yeah," Tammy agreed turning around in the seat and looking back at the trailer.

Not having experience with travel trailers, I didn't recognize the seriousness of the problem and kept driving. Not far away, the road turned into a four-lane highway and I looked cautiously for a spot to pull out as traffic whizzed by at a rapid pace.

A few hundred yards down the highway, the car lurched violently forward and the trailer suddenly snapped free. The Cadillac was already in the left-hand lane and, before I knew it, the runaway trailer had passed us headed down the right-hand lane.

"Oh, my God," I whispered.

Tammy started praying in tongues immediately. Beads of perspiration popped out on my forehead as I swerved from one lane to another as the trailer crisscrossed the highway.

Up ahead, a roadside diner loomed. The trailer was heading straight for the restaurant. It was around suppertime and I knew the little diner would be filled with people.

Tears stained my cheeks as I cried out, "Oh God, please help us!"

Without warning, the trailer suddenly whipped off the road, slammed into a utility pole, and split in half. The twisted hunk of metal that once was our new trailer was a total loss. A few moments before it had been gleaming and shining in the setting sun . . . and now it was just a piece of rubble.

Miraculously, our musical equipment was untouched!

On the Road for Jesus

The state patrol arrived quickly and tried to find out what had happened from two badly-shaken people. Tammy was in tears. "I just can't believe God would allow this."

I felt the same way, yet I knew God wouldn't allow it unless He had something better in mind. "Honey," I said putting my arm around her waist, "I know this looks awful but God's got to bring good out of it somehow. I don't know how. I'm just believing He will."

I quickly phoned the pastor of the church where we were scheduled to minister the next day. It was already dark when he arrived to pick us up and we were exhausted from the experience.

His church had always been known on the evangelistic circuit as a hard one for a revival. His people were reserved and staid. The next morning, Sunday, the revival started and it was a tough day for us. We were reaching out to new people in a new place and we were still badly shaken by the loss of our new trailer.

But we got ready for the service anyway. Tammy began the service by singing "How Big Is God." She had sung only a verse when, too choked to continue, she laid her head on her accordion and began sobbing.

Not knowing about our trailer wreck, the congregation rustled uneasily.

I stood up saying, "You'll have to excuse Tammy this morning folks. We've just gone through something and it's a little overwhelming."

Tears began flowing from my own eyes as I tried to explain about the trailer. "God has been so good to us. We have been on the evangelistic field over three years moving from town to town. Several weeks ago He provided over fifteen hundred dollars for us to purchase a new travel trailer. Yesterday, that new trailer ended up wrapped around a utility pole on the highway."

All over the auditorium, ladies popped open their purses in search of tissues while men coughed uncomfortably in the sensitive atmosphere.

I walked down from the pulpit to the altar. "Lord," I said with my arms raised in the air, "I don't know what you have in mind but I give up. I surrender to your will." And with that I knelt at the altar and began weeping.

The strains of organ music flowed throughout the sanctuary as I heard what seemed like hundreds of steps behind me. People were on their knees in tears all around the altar. Grown men leaned over the pews and wept. Whole families joined together at the altar.

Unbelievable revival broke out. Young people came forward and gave their hearts to the Lord, older folks got their hearts of stone softened by the Holy Spirit, and healings were reported by the score before that Sunday morning service had ended. Our trailer had not been wrecked in vain.

Actually we hadn't wanted that particular model of a trailer anyway because it had square corners and fought the wind traveling down the road. We had wanted one of the new rounded edge ones, but they were a month away from coming out when we purchased ours. But when we checked into why the trailer had snapped free from the car, the dealer admitted spot welding on the hitch had been the cause.

Thus the company replaced the trailer free! And to top it off, we ended up with a rounded edge trailer for the same price. In the face of what looked like disaster, God had worked everything to our good.

We had been traveling some time on the circuit when we realized we needed to make a change. Our approach appealed to adults and teenagers, but not much to the smaller kids.

One day at a grocery store I was struggling up the aisle with a loaded cart when I found Tammy standing around the corner looking at some bubble bath containers. "What are you doing?" I asked.

"Jim, I've got an idea."

"Well, what is it?"

"See these little animal heads on top of the bubble bath cartons?" I nodded.

"Well, if we melt down the ears, put a tiny wig on it, repaint the face, what do you think we'll have?"

"What?"

"Puppets."

"Puppets?"

"Sure, don't you see? These little animals have holes in the bottom that you can put your fingers in to operate the puppet's head."

"Well, that's great, but then what do we do with them?"

"Listen, silly, we use them for children. Haven't we been looking for something for children?"

"Of course!"

With that we bought ten cartons of bubble bath and hurried off to see what we could create with them. The result was Susie Moppet and her family: Billy, Johnny, Dad, Grandpa, Grandma, Mom. We decided to act out stories with moral lessons using the puppets. Tammy had a perfect voice for Susie and several of the characters, but we'd need most of the voices on tape so that we could operate the puppets, and I had recently given away my tape recorder to a missionary group in Africa.

We took the matter to the Lord. Some time passed and we still were not able to use the puppets for lack of a tape recorder. However, at a certain meeting we were conducting, a young man who had been saved earlier in the week came up to me as the service ended.

"Jim, can you use a tape recorder?"

"How did you know?"

"I didn't. But I bought a brand new tape recorder—I didn't even know why—which I'm still making payments on. Now it seems that the Lord wants me to give it to you."

While he walked out to his car for the tape recorder, I sat down on a nearby pew and marveled. It seemed the lessons in faith never ended.

The following week we began using the puppets in a church at Rockville, Maryland. Almost immediately it was a success. Kids were enthralled by Susie Moppet and her family. I built a small wooden stage and Tammy used her portable sewing machine to make the stage's drapes. From the very start kids couldn't seem to get enough of the puppets.

Near the end of that week in Rockville, I was upstairs resting one afternoon when the telephone rang. Tammy answered and began motioning to me, "Honey, it's your daddy and he sounds upset."

"Daddy, what seems to be the problem? Are you okay?"

"Yes, but I had to call to let you know that Grandma Irwin passed away."

"Grandma Irwin's dead?"

"Yes, she's gone home to be with the Lord."

I hung up the phone and walked over to the window. Across the street children were playing in a park. They shouted, screamed and laughed at one another as they played. Light fluffy clouds floated overhead in the clear blue sky.

But inside my world was different. The person who had stood by me and loved me most when I was walking in darkness was gone. A feeling of bitterness began to settle over me. Somehow it made me mad. Mad at a system called death. . . .

Tammy interrupted my thoughts. "Jim, remember, your father said Grandma Irwin hadn't even been ill."

I thought for a few moments. "I guess you're right," I said softly. "She loved all of us, but she loved Jesus more."

"Jim, I think we should do something special in honor of Grandma Irwin at the revival."

I felt a gentle peace as Tammy spoke. "You're right,

48

honey. I don't think we should go back to Muskegon for the funeral. She would have wanted us to stay and go on with the services.''

And that's what we did. Tammy sang more beautifully than I'd ever heard her, and God anointed my preaching as never before. The meeting was a glorious salute to Grandma Irwin.

5

Number One
Crawford Parkway

Why can't Christians have a talk show, too?'' I shouted to
Tammy as she prepared our late night snack in the kitchen of our
trailer.

She came to the door, ''What are you talking about?''

I'm talking about these late night talk shows,'' I pointed to
the television set. ''For years I've been coming home from meetings at night when these shows are on with movie stars talking
about their latest love affairs.''

Tammy shook her head. ''I don't know the answer,'' she
said, heading back to the kitchen to finish the sandwiches.

I sat on the couch and thought about it. Since I had been
traveling as an evangelist I would come home from the services
and try to unwind before going to sleep. Eating a snack and
watching some television was always a comfortable way to unwind, but at that time of the night the only things being telecast
were two late night talk shows and a movie.

''Lord, maybe it's just me,'' I prayed, ''but it seems like

there ought to be some kind of talk show for Christians. I'm sure there are a lot of people who need You at this hour of the night.''

Tammy and I thought we would be on the evangelistic field for the rest of our lives. Many larger churches were now opening their doors to us and we were beginning to travel all over the southeastern United States.

Not only did God continue bringing the exciting results of souls being saved, healed and delivered—he continued blessing us in the small ways. Once outside a small church, a man walked up to me, ''Jim, I've been looking at your front tires and they're not going to make it much farther.''

''Thanks I didn't realize that.''

He flashed a warm smile, ''Don't worry about it. I own a place in town and I'll fix them up for you.'' Next day, he did that. But instead of two tires, he gave us four brand new ones.

After four years on the evangelistic circuit, I began to see that in going from one church to another, I was reaching the same crowd the last evangelist reached. And they all wanted me to preach better than the last evangelist preached. But, if you preached too well, the pastor sometimes became jealous. On the other hand, if you didn't preach well enough they wouldn't like that either. All in all, I began to feel strained.

During the spring of 1965, we were conducting a revival for Gordon Churchill who was pastoring a church in the Tidewater area of Virginia. I had come to know and love the area since we had been holding some twelve revivals a year there.

Gordon was working part-time as a radio announcer at WXRI, which he described as a Christian radio station. ''They also have a Christian television station broadcasting over Channel 27,'' he said. ''The only problem is that they desperately need new programs.''

''It sounds like a good way to reach people for the Lord,'' I observed.

Number One Crawford Parkway

Gordon sat straight up in his chair. "Say, why don't we go down to the station and talk with Bill Garthwaite? They've been looking for somebody to do a children's program. Maybe you can help them."

"Why not? I don't know anything about television, but I have worked with kids."

Bill Garthwaite was at the station when Gordon and I arrived, and he seemed eager for someone to do a kids' show. "I'm not concerned about your lack of experience in broadcasting, Jim," he said. "I think your puppets would more than offset that. Kids are always interested in puppets."

With Bill's help, we quickly put together a special children's show. The show ran quite smoothly and, as we went off the air, the station's switchboard put through a call to me. Tammy and I were excited thinking somebody had actually liked the show.

Instead, it was a woman from a church where we had previously held revival services, "I just wanted to let you know that if you don't stop working with those silly puppets, you'll end up losing your entire ministry."

"Yes, ma'am," I answered dejectedly. "Thank you for calling."

Following that phone call, I put away any interest in television. But after getting back on the road, I began receiving letters from Pat Robertson who was head of the Christian television station back in Portsmouth. Pat was looking for somebody to do a regular children's show. Bill Garthwaite had been impressed with our hastily-produced program and he had recommended us.

My first reaction to his letters was "no." After four years on the road, we were finally getting to the place where we weren't struggling to make ends meet and I hated the thought of leaving. My "no" letter to Pat Robertson prompted him to write and invite us to visit him the next time we were in the area to talk about it.

Several months later we were back in the Tidewater area,

but had forgotten about Pat Robertson and his Christian station. Pat, however, had not forgotten us and he called to take Tammy and me out to lunch.

After lunch, we took a tour of the shabby, rundown studios he was grandly calling the Christian Broadcasting Network. Located in a poor section of Portsmouth, the station was housed in a broken-down building that looked to be splitting apart. The building sat on the bank of a small creek and, from a distance, it looked as though half of it was trying to slide into the water while the other half was desperately clinging to the bank.

Somehow, I just couldn't connect Pat Robertson with this ramshackle building. The son of Virginia's senior U.S. Senator, Pat looked every inch a senator himself. His vision of carrying the gospel into all the world through broadcasting was a contagious thing. Before I knew it, I was getting excited hearing him discuss the endless possibilities of Christian broadcasting . . . and he shared how, by miracle after miracle, God had raised up the ministry.

Settling into Pat's car in the dusty parking lot off Spratley Street, we prayed. Tammy and I both felt that this was what God wanted us to do.

"Pat," I said after a long silence, "we 'll come and work for you on one condition."

"What's that?"

I looked him square in the face, "We'll do a children's program, but I also want to do a late night talk show one day. The talk show is very important to me and has been for a long time."

"Okay," he responded, "we'll get the kids show started first. Then, later on, you can do the talk show."

We finished our tour of meetings in the weeks immediately following, and then I canceled almost a year's worth of meetings, the cream of the revivals we had been working up to. After a brief visit with our families, we left for Portsmouth. It was September 1965.

Number One Crawford Parkway

Arriving in town, I knew we couldn't live in the travel trailer, so I made arrangements to sell it. I also decided if we were going to be working for the Lord in the community, we should live somewhere nice. Out driving one day, I noticed some high rise apartments near the Elizabeth River.

Pulling up to Number One Crawford Parkway, I thought to myself, "Can we afford this?"

A doorman opened our car door and we walked into a chandelier-draped lobby. "I'd like to see one of your apartments," I said to the resident manager. Inside I was having more doubts about being able to afford the place . . . for all I knew these apartments could have been six or seven hundred dollars a month, and we were only making a hundred and fifty a week. Yet, I felt God leading us here.

The gray-haired matron must have known exactly what we could afford. She led us upstairs and showed us an efficiency apartment. Like all the other apartments, it had a large living room and a balcony with a sweeping view of the Elizabeth River. The only difference with this unit was that there was no bedroom.

"What is the rent here?" I asked casually looking out the wide sliding glass doors leading to the balcony.

"A hundred and fifty a month."

"Fine, we'll take it."

We never told anyone the apartment didn't have a bedroom. With so many doors opening off the huge living room, everybody probably thought the door leading to the furnace was our bedroom. We purchased a comfortable hide-a-bed and that worked out fine until the Lord could perform another miracle with accommodations.

One day Tammy was taking the elevator up to our apartment. "And what floor do you live on?" a society matron asked with her nose pointed high in the air.

"The seventh," Tammy hung her head slightly.

"We live on the eighteenth," the woman said tartly.

The eighteenth floor was the most expensive in the high rise. We were perfectly satisfied in our efficiency on the seventh floor, but within a year God had changed our financial situation so radically that we were able to move to the eighteenth floor ourselves.

Then when the society matrons would ask Tammy, "And what floor do you live on?" she could say, "Praise God, we've gone to eighteen."

I wasn't a broadcasting professional but even I could see that the station's equipment was in terrible shape. The studio itself was dirty and almost always either too hot or cold. Field mice frequently ran around the place (much to Tammy's consternation). Our first office had been the chief engineer's storeroom and we hauled garbage and greasy equipment out for several days before turning the place into a habitable spot.

The station was only broadcasting a few hours daily when we first arrived. A news program, a country and western show, and our children's show were the basic programming fare for the day. Our first show was called "Come On Over." Before the show started, Tammy cried all night long. She just couldn't believe we could ever come up with any kind of program that people, especially kids, would watch.

"I just can't go through with it," she sobbed.

"Honey," I said, trying to encourage her, "yes you can, with God's help."

She still wasn't convinced. "Do you believe the Lord brought us here?" I asked. She nodded in agreement. "Well then, let's trust the Lord for whatever He wants to do."

Tammy was still jittery the next day, but she was at least prepared to do the show. That afternoon, we went through the neighborhood around the station gathering kids to appear on the first program. I had already built the first set for the show. It was a white frame house with a front porch where Tammy and I would make our grand entrance. Then I added some nearby bleachers for the kids.

Surprisingly, while I was relaxed on my first appearance on television, Tammy— who had been very comfortable in front of people at our revivals—froze up when the camera closed in on her. I finally had to rescue the microphone and introduce her.

Unknown to us, CBN was already in deep financial waters when we arrived that September. But God began using "Come On Over" to help reverse that situation almost immediately.

Kids who had been fooling with the television dial found the show and started watching. Soon their parents began to watch. That first week we got ten or fifteen letters in the mail. In 1965 that was unheard of.

Each night we would have about fifty kids in the studio audience. They got there by writing for tickets. Being a "live" program five nights a week, the studio was constantly filled with these youngsters milling all over the building with their parents.

When Halloween neared, I announced plans for a big party at the studio. Hundreds of kids swarmed into the station. From that point on, we recognized our growth potential among the kids.

By November, the CBN financial picture was still bleak, and plans were made for its first big telethon to reach a budget of $10,000 a month. Two years earlier Pat had gone on the air with CBN's first telethon, and the Lord had provided 700 faith partners who supported the ministry with ten dollars apiece each month. From this the telethon was dubbed the "700 Club" and several telephones were installed so people could call in their pledges for 1966. Guests were invited to sing and give their testimonies while the telephone pledges were being recorded.

Tony Fontaine, a former nightclub and recording star from Hollywood, had agreed to participate in the telethon which had been scheduled over a weekend. Everybody worked hard during the telethon, but by Sunday night we were far short of our $120,000 yearly goal.

Before going on the air, the staff had been instructed not to tell the viewing audience that CBN was in financial trouble. The station was over $40,000 in debt.

That kind of approach didn't make sense to me. By now, I was fully committed to Christian television and felt that if I didn't tell people the truth, there wouldn't be any Christian television around. If we didn't meet the goal, the station would be forced to close down.

Near the end of the telethon, while I was on camera, I broke down and began crying. I had tried to hold my feelings back, but finally I was overwhelmed with the burden of the situation.

"Our entire purpose has been to serve the Lord Jesus Christ through radio and television," I said, "but we've fallen far short. We need $10,000 a month or we'll be off the air."

I could feel the tears freely running down my cheeks and dropping from my face, but I couldn't help myself.

"Listen people," I said, "it's all over. Everything's gone. Christian television will be no more. The only Christian television station is gone, unless you provide us with the money to operate it."

Almost instantly, the phones in the studio began ringing and, soon, all ten lines were jammed. People had been touched by the Spirit of God.

Very shortly after that the small studio began filling up with people who couldn't reach us by telephone. Some were crying. Others were bawling. Most of them had money in their hands. It was almost 2:30 a.m. before we signed off the air, our studio still packed with God's people who had rallied to the cause.

All the back bills were paid and our next year's budget was fully underwritten. And yet God wasn't finished. Monday morning the phones began ringing again. People were pledging more support. On Tuesday and Wednesday, however, the nature of the nearly incessant calls began to change. In addition to pledging support, people asked us to pray with them for healing, help and guidance. The telephone volunteers prayed, and reported that miracles were happening.

John Carraway, a Baptist minister on the staff, answered one of the phones and led a family of nine people to Christ. Pat prayed with a small child who had a horrible scar on her face. Her excited grandmother called back minutes later to say God had wiped it off her face.

The CBN ministry was now free to move further on into God's plan.

The next year, Stuart Hamblen, the gifted songwriter who had been converted in Billy Graham's famous Los Angeles crusade of 1949, was the telethon's special guest. CBN's budget this time had risen to $150,000 a year, but we needed an additional $30,000 down payment to purchase a new transmitter.

Once again, viewers flooded the station with telephone calls and prayer requests. Twelve phone lines were tied up almost constantly by thousands of requests. By Sunday night, God had raised the entire budget plus the additional money for the transmitter.

The next day the staff met to pray and everyone agreed that we should continue the program each night. The station already had attracted the interest of the people, and we needed another program to fill our format. Since Pat had begun the telethons as the "700 Club Telethon," it was decided to call the nightly program the "700 Club."

Pat agreed to let me develop the program into a late-night talk show, as he had promised. The show came on at ten o'clock on November 28, 1966. The program was a team effort, even though I was acting as host. The telethon volunteers were still sitting behind a bank of phones.

I picked Matthew 18:19 as the theme scripture for the show: ". . . if two of you shall agree on earth as touching any thing that they shall ask, it shall be done for them of my Father which is in heaven."

In those early days, we had a problem finding guests since we had to depend entirely on local personalities and ministers coming through Portsmouth. Some nights I actually resorted to interviewing a cameraman. Then I began to depend more on the Lord to supply the guests. Many times we were right up to air time and somebody would walk in. In fact some of the best programs came when God sent a guest at the last minute.

While I interviewed guests or we listened to them sing, viewers with spiritual, physical or other needs would call in their requests. The phones ringing in the background added a special touch to the broadcast. When an answer to prayer was reported or someone was led to Jesus over the phone, the Spirit of God seemed to become more real in the studio.

I hadn't planned to do any radio work when I first joined CBN, but we needed an announcer. So I studied for my third-class operator's license and began doing a daily radio shift. Since the "700 Club" was simultaneously being broadcast over radio and television, I would often announce the program over radio, race into the television studio and leap behind the desk, just in time to begin hosting the show. Afterwards, I would make the return trip to the radio booth to close out the show.

It was my work on CBN's radio station, WXRI, which occasioned my first serious problem at the network.

At the time I was doing a radio shift, the children's show, and hosting the "700 Club," which many times ran into the early hours of the morning. I was practically working night and day since the staff was short-handed.

Unknown to me, Jay Arlan, the radio station's manager, had asked several announcers to take a Saturday night shift. Nobody could handle the extra shift, so he finally came to me. "Jim, I want you to work Saturday night," he said.

"I'm sorry, Jay," I answered. "I can't do it this Saturday

night. I've promised to take Tammy out. I've been up to my ears in work and we haven't been out together for months.''

"Well," Jay said, "you still have to do it."

I shook my head. "Jay, I can't."

And that's the way I left it. Jay was the manager of the radio station and I figured he would either get somebody else or do the shift himself. But that night, while Tammy and I drove home from dinner in Norfolk, I clicked the radio on to WXRI. There was nothing but silence on the air. Nobody had showed up to do the shift, and the announcer from the previous shift simply shut the transmitter down and went home.

The next day blame for the entire situation had been laid at my doorstep. Pat Robertson called me into his office. I explained that since my basic job was in television, I was just helping out as a radio announcer. On top of that, I had told the station manager I couldn't make the schedule.

"Jim, I don't have any choice," Pat finally said. "We've established a chain of command, and you've broken it. I've got to uphold discipline and have no choice but to make you an example. You have to choose. You can pay a $100 fine or you can resign."

"Pat, I've been here long enough that if you feel I need disciplining in front of the whole organization, I guess I'm finished here."

Getting up from my chair I mumbled, "Good-bye, Pat," and walked out the door. Tammy and I picked up the puppets and a few of our belongings, and left the studios. John Gilman temporarily took over the children's show, and that night we sat home watching the program and weeping.

By the end of the week, I put out a fleece to God—"I will go back to work at CBN if Pat Robertson himself asks me."

Several days later, I made my last trip to the studio to pick up a few remaining personal items. Pat called me into his office.

Shutting the door behind me he said, "Jim, I want you to come back."

Inwardly I breathed a sigh of relief. "God has been dealing with me," I responded, "and I don't think I should leave. I've never been more miserable in all my life."

Pulling two fifty-dollar bills from his pocket, Pat said, "I'll pay your fine, Jim."

"Thanks, Pat," I said. I paid my fine and Tammy and I went back to work.

After that experience I felt much closer to Pat. He had performed a Christlike act by paying the very fine he had levied on me. Even more, I knew he had obeyed the voice of the Lord by asking me to come back. That meant a great deal and I committed myself to working diligently for the Lord at CBN. I believed totally that we were exactly where God wanted us to be.

6

The Jim and Tammy Show

From the moment that I stepped before a television camera at CBN, God began to anoint me to raise money for Christian television. I realized it the night I wept during the first "700 Club" telethon. Many times since then, God similarly anointed me.

But one August night in 1967, while hosting the "700 Club," I felt the Lord urging me to raise money for CBN to purchase color cameras. Earlier Pat and I had talked about the station going color. He told me that RCA had two 141-C color cameras, the last two of that model, and would sell them for $70,000. Normally, a single 141-C sold for $70,000. We could have them for half price.

The only problem: we had to have a ten percent down payment within twenty-four hours to hold the cameras. I went on the air that night and presented it to the people. The viewing audience responded generously and, before the show left the air, the down payment had been raised.

That night 180 miles away in Goldsboro, North Carolina, Henry Harrison, a veteran of some twenty years in broadcasting, was listening to the program over radio. Having received the Baptism in the Holy Spirit under Pat Robertson's ministry, Henry decided to make a contribution toward the cameras. Since he didn't know anyone at CBN other than Pat, he placed a long distance, person-to-person call to the station and wound up talking to Pat at home.

Totally unaware of events at the station, Pat sleepily answered the phone and thanked Henry for his call. "I feel the Lord is leading me into full-time Christian ministry," Henry said, "and I wonder if there might be something at CBN that I could do."

Knowing Henry's substantial background in broadcasting, Pat shouted, "Praise God, brother. This is an answer to prayer. We've been praying for someone to take over the radio work. We've just lost two people."

Within a few days Henry was in Portsmouth and Pat hired him. Later he came down to the studio where I was working with the production crew. When I met this smiling, robust man, it was like David and Jonathan, our souls were knit together.

"Henry," I said, "I'm so excited about you coming here to work that I hate to see you leave for the trip home, even though I know you're coming right back."

Henry laughed, "I know what you mean, brother."

Not only did Henry join CBN as the radio station's manager, we also created a role for him on the children's show, which we had renamed the "Jim and Tammy Show." The name "Tammy" was being widely used in movies and popular songs and we were advised a name-change would help the show. It worked well because Tammy's fresh good looks and colorful disposition with the children had made her an immediate favorite with our viewers.

Henry Harrison became "Uncle Henry" on the show. He was the owner of a general store where the puppets did their shopping from time to time. Being from the country, "Uncle

Henry'' dressed in a wide straw hat, large bib overalls and heavy brogans. Occasionally he even brought various animals into the studio, as well as vegetables from the farm.

Henry lived with us temporarily when he first joined CBN, and later, when he married, I was best man at his wedding. His bride joined our children's program as "Aunt Susan." With her old-fashioned bonnet and gingham dress, she became a lovable addition to the team.

Everyone who worked on the show became deeply involved. The crew members often dreamt up stunts to pull on me during the show—and I was generally a little nervous through the program waiting for the stunt to appear. One night I began talking about all the mail that arrived daily at the studio, when someone standing behind the set dumped a barrel full of it over my head!

Another time, I was opening the mailbox to read letters to the children, not knowing that the mailbox had been spring-loaded. When I opened the lid, mail shot all over the studio narrowly missing my head. But without the aid of writers or producers, we had developed great interplay between crew and cast.

Ricky Milan, Walt Mills, Freddy House and Dale Hill all were responsible for the show's tremendous reception by the viewing audience. The crew always became involved with the activity on camera. During one show I said, "Beauty is only skin deep," and Freddy quipped from behind the camera, "Yeah, but ugly goes clear to the bone!"

The cameramen decorated their cameras during Christmas and Halloween, and when we participated in local parades they joined in decorating the floats. Almost without exception, our floats won first place every time. Our personal appearances at shopping centers and civic auditoriums even outdrew Santa Claus. Once when we were scheduled to appear at the Norfolk Civic Auditorium, the place was packed an hour before the show and we ultimately had to do two performances.

Move That Mountain

What with doing a "live" show five days a week without a script, it wasn't too surprising that some of the programs didn't come together particularly well. One night I recognized the program just wasn't jelling. It was dull. Before I knew it, I found myself saying, "This show is bad. Let's start all over again."

Dale Hill, the show's director who had joined CBN a few years before while still attending high school, was always alert on the set and immediately went to black on the screen, cued the slide and began playing the show's theme song again. Tammy and I hurried to our positions and walked out the front door of the house with . . . "Hi, boys and girls. We're so glad to have you over. Welcome to the Jim and Tammy Show again."

Unbelievably, the "live" show went perfectly the second time around.

Sometimes we tried to plan humorous moments. Other times the fun came unexpectedly. One of the regular features of the show was interviewing the kids. I would introduce them and maybe ask a question or two. Once we had the son of our chief engineer on the program.

"Folks," I said, "this is Kevin, the son of our fine chief engineer, Bill Gregory." Kevin gave the camera a wide grin.

"Kevin," I asked lightly, "what did your mother and daddy tell you before you came on the show today?"

Kevin eyed me seriously before he replied, "They told me not to cuss."

The camera focused on me. "Well, that's our chief engineer's son," I deadpanned.

On another occasion, we were reading helpful hints that we had asked the children to write in. We called this segment "mail time." Someone had written, "If you take soap out of the package as soon as you get it the cake will dry out and last twice as long."

Tammy commented, "That reminds me of what my Aunt Gin used to do."

"What's that?"

"She used to unwrap cakes of soap and put them in her drawers," Tammy said innocently.

Everybody in the studio started snickering—especially our crew.

Tammy saw what was happening and she tried to explain herself . . . "No, you don't understand. . . ." The whole place erupted in loud guffaws and Tammy blushed bright red. For the remainder of the show, everything seemed to revolve around Tammy's revelation about her Aunt Gin.

Another time Tammy and I planned to do a "take-off" on a regular television commercial. The studio and viewing audiences wouldn't suspect anything because we did have a few regular commercials in those days. We had an artist draw up a sign advertising "Stoneware China for $29.95" and we stacked a pile of plates on a counter. Tammy had laughed every time she tried to run through the commercial and I had to rehearse her until she wouldn't laugh.

That night she played the commercial straight through without a giggle. At the end she said, "Just to prove how durable this china is, I'll drop it on the floor." She took a pile of the plates and dropped them on some metal weights on the floor, breaking the dishes into hundreds of pieces.

Nobody thought it was funny. The kids didn't laugh. Tammy didn't laugh. The crew was silent.

Dale tried to salvage the mess by ringing our little play telephone on the set. I picked it up and pretended to speak to the show's sponsor. "Yes sir," I said apologetically, "I know the plates broke. I'm terribly sorry."

By then Tammy was almost in tears over the scene. A few people actually called the station later to sympathize with Tammy, still unaware that the whole thing was supposed to be a joke. Afterwards our whole staff had a big laugh over the fractured commercial that failed. We had an even bigger laugh when we discovered Stoneware China was a real product and we could have been sued for making fun of it!

"The Jim and Tammy Show" was a big party for the kids, but all the fun was eventually geared to winning these same kids to Jesus. We brought them Bible stories and Christian lessons through the fun and games which let them know that Christianity is a great way to live. Christianity had been portrayed as dull and dour by so many television shows; we felt the "Jim and Tammy Show" presented a different image.

7

"The Spirit is Moving . . ."

Even though I was hosting the "700 Club," as production manager I worked right along with the crews. Many times I would climb up a shaky ladder to adjust the lights before I sat down behind the desk to host the show.

"It's a good thing we don't have smell-o-vision," I said one day while attempting to replace some lights in the dirt and grime of the studio's rigging. I was dripping from head to toe with sweat and smelled like a spoiled mackerel.

Since the "700 Club" was the last program of the day, there was no time limit to the show. If God was truly moving, we could stay on until two o'clock in the morning . . . and sometimes we did.

One night the countdown to sign off was under way with less than sixty seconds remaining, when I heard God say: *You have not drawn the net.*

Immediately I realized that the program had awakened a desire for salvation in the hearts of many viewers, but I had not offered an invitation to receive Jesus. "We can't go off," I shouted to the crew. "God isn't finished."

I proceeded to give a simple invitation. Eleven people quickly responded to it and then the program closed.

In the beginning, the "700 Club's" basic message was salvation and we kept discreetly quiet about the Baptism with the Holy Spirit and speaking in tongues. But one night, late in 1967, the emphasis began to shift dramatically. It was a typical program complete with singing groups and interviews until the last fifteen minutes.

Construction work was under way for our new studios and temporary rigging was hanging in place among an inch or two of construction dirt. Most of the other groups had already left the studio when the Cameron Family Singers from Scotland came on. The presence of the Holy Spirit began to intensify in the studio.

"All over the world, the Spirit is moving . . ." the group was singing when Wendy Cameron, wife of the group's leader, Simon Peter, began dancing in the Spirit. As she danced, her face was transfigured.

Heaven itself seemed to descend into the studio and the show continued until five o'clock in the morning. The Camerons sang and gave their testimonies. Telephones began ringing to report healings and miracles throughout the Tidewater area.

Simon Peter, a burly, redheaded Scotsman, began giving his testimony of having been converted from alcoholism. Tears stained his face as he told of returning from World War II as a drunkard and finding his wife a Christian. "For the next seven years I worked to break her spirit," he confessed, "and I failed."

"One day at work I broke down and began crying. I couldn't stop. I wept so uncontrollably that fellow workers had to take me home. And in the stillness of my home, I knelt and asked Jesus into my heart. I prayed, 'Jesus, take me' . . . and He did!"

Hundreds of people phoned to give their hearts to the Lord while Simon Peter wept his testimony over the airwaves. Once he finished his story he began preaching about the victorious life through Christ. From time to time, I ran in to interrupt him with reports about miracles in the viewing audience.

God was rousing people from their sleep to turn on their televisions. Many people called their neighbors and told them about the all-night program. Others dressed hurriedly and came down to the studio to see what was happening.

By five o'clock, hundreds of people had called the station to say they had given their hearts to Christ. My voice had grown hoarse through the night—yet I was thrilled.

That morning when Tammy and I finally left the studio, the devil began saying: "You're going to be the laughing stock of Portsmouth." And for the first time I began to wonder how people would react to what had happened that night on the program.

After getting some sleep, I drove to the bank to make a deposit. "Say," the man behind the counter said, "that was the most beautiful program I've ever seen. I've never felt the presence of the Lord as much as last night."

Later I turned into a service station for gasoline. "Aren't you on Channel 27?" the man asked while wiping the windshield. "Yes," I smiled.

"Well, I just want you to know," he said returning the smile, "I was up all last night with you and I really enjoyed it."

It seemed everybody we met that day had stayed up the night before watching the program. God had given us a mighty miracle . . . and the devil had been proven a liar once again.

Early in 1968, CBN went on the air with a telethon called "New Continents for Christ" in hopes of raising $25,000 for the purchase of a radio station in Bogota, Colombia. Pat told the television audience of his concern for missions and asked them to believe that God would supply the needed funds.

Late Sunday night, I was on camera when we reached the goal. "We've done it," I shouted. "We're over the goal. We've raised the money for Nuevo Continente!" As I spoke, a stormy gust of wind lifted our unfinished studio's roof sending a section of decking onto the floor below.

"Everybody run for your lives," I screamed into the camera, "the roof's falling in." People were running and screaming in all directions. "It's an explosion from the devil to show his displeasure that we're moving into Bogota," I shouted. With the ceiling falling in, we were suddenly knocked off the air. It was the most remarkable ending to a telethon I have ever seen.

Within a few months our new studios were completed and we were broadcasting from them. Our first prayer for those new facilities was that the glory of God would fill them so that anyone who walked into the place would feel the Lord's presence.

One night, during the "700 Club," the Holy Spirit's presence came in a dramatic way. I could feel the holiness of God in the studio and I heard the voice of the Lord saying, *Take off your shoes, you're on holy ground.*

I spoke the words in obedience and soon everybody in the studio began removing their shoes. Giving the microphone to Pat, I said, "I'm going to pray." Stepping off camera, I lifted my hands in praise and began worshipping the Lord in the Spirit.

Pat kept trying to get me back on camera, but I was lost in the heavenlies with Jesus. "I don't want to come back, I don't want to come back," I repeated over and over.

He finally looked into the cameras saying, "God has told me to get out of the way, and I don't know what to do or where to go. I don't want to block His power."

Finally he handed the microphone to Lee Russell, a talented singer formerly with the Vincent Lopez orchestra. "Brother, sing something so I can get out of the way," Pat suggested. As Lee began to sing, the feeling of God's presence became so strong in the studio that people in every corner of the building began weeping. Two cameramen huddled arm-in-arm around a camera, weeping until a puddle of water formed under their feet.

The people in the control booth were crying so uncontrollably they couldn't operate the equipment. They just set the controls on automatic. Cameramen couldn't see through the lenses of their cameras. Directors could no longer give instructions. There was nobody left to run the station's equipment and finally we had to go off the air.

The last shot that night was a wide angle view of the entire set—empty. The cameras had been locked in place and the entire staff was off the set sobbing and weeping in God's presence. The entire staff huddled on the studio's floor arm-in-arm and wept before the Lord. It was a genuine revival among CBN's staff, the likes of which nobody had ever seen.

At times it seemed the healing power of God was moving in trends. One night it might be cataracts. The next night it would be deafness. In some cases we wouldn't even be praying for some of the sicknesses, and yet the testimonies would suddenly pour into the station. Healings for blindness, arthritis, lameness were constantly being reported.

One night over twenty-five people called to praise God because they had been healed from some form of deafness. It was as if God was saying *I'm with you, but I'm healing as I will.*

Another night, a man fatally ill with leukemia was watching the program. Strangely the Lord led me to pray: "In the name of Jesus . . . in the name of Jesus . . . in the name of Jesus, be healed." For over a year I never understood why God led me to pray in that way until, one day, that man walked into the studios. "I just wanted you to know," he said with a gleam in his eyes, "I have a positive release from my doctor. I was healed a year ago when you prayed and each time you said, 'In the name of Jesus,' a warmth went through a third of my body."

The Lord never ceased to amaze me with the countless ways He brought healings to people. On another occasion I was challenging folks to believe God for healing. "You go," I urged, "and lay hands on your children, or any sick person in your home. Pray for them and God will answer."

A ten-year-old boy was watching with his parents. In another room, a younger sister born with club feet was asleep. He quietly slipped into her room and prayed for her. "My little sister's healed," he announced, walking back into the living room. "That's nice," they answered, trying to humor him.

But the next morning when the little girl got out of bed, her feet were perfectly normal. As Mark 16:18 declared ". . . they shall lay hands on the sick, and they shall recover."

Then there was the night we were preparing for a telethon. The Downings, a popular singing group, and a large choir were appearing on the program and I was serving as emcee.

It was just a few minutes before air time and the technicians were going through their last microphone checks and lighting adjustments.

I was standing to one side of the set when Paul Downing, the group's leader, walked up. Paul suffered periodically from a facial paralysis known as "Bell's palsy" and, sure enough, his face was badly distorted. Half of it looked normal while the other half seemed almost grotesque. His right eye appeared about ready to fall from its socket.

"Jim," he said pitifully through a thick, half-paralyzed tongue, "the doctors have said I've got to stop singing. I'll have to give up traveling with the group . . . this condition has been going on for months and it's getting worse."

Something inside of me seemed to cry out as Paul spoke.

". . . please remember to pray for me," he said.

Reaching out for his hands, I responded, "Paul, let's pray right now."

Paul nodded. "In the name of Jesus," I prayed, "be healed!"

He jerked backwards momentarily, and, before my eyes, Paul's face returned to normal, instantaneously!

"The Spirit is Moving . . ."

The place suddenly went into a buzz. People were shouting and praising God as Paul danced around the studio. "It's gone! It's gone! I can feel my face again," he cried.

That night instead of a routine telethon, we had revival.

8

Through the Valley of Nerves

Tammy and I liked to think we were an average married couple, but two "live" television shows five nights a week brought incredible pressure to bear on our lives. Not only were there the two shows, but I also worked on the fund-raising telethons and other areas of CBN's ministry.

Frequently the only time we had available to talk was just before the kids' show went on the air. When Tammy was upset with me, or I with her, it was especially tough since we had to spend the next hour or so in front of a tale-telling camera and try to act civil toward one another.

When Tammy couldn't express her emotions any other way, she would do it through Susie Moppet. Once, after introducing Susie to the kids, I asked, "And how are you tonight, Susie Moppet?"

"I feel just awful," Susie replied with Tammy's voice . . . and for the next few minutes Susie raked me over the hot coals much to the delight of the kids. And of course, Tammy enjoyed it, too. I guess, looking back now, I really deserved it.

Move That Mountain

One night in May 1969, four years of long hours and constant pressures—which I had tried so hard to ignore—finally caught up with me. After finishing the "700 Club," I went home and collapsed. A wave of dizziness swept over me as I tried to rest in bed and my stomach finally erupted in continual vomiting.

By morning, I could hardly lift my weary body out of the bed. My nerves were jangled and I felt as though I was losing all the restraints that held my life together. I couldn't even bear to talk with anyone. I wanted only to be away from people.

Tammy's eyes told me she was frightened by my condition. "Honey," she said with tears beginning to form in her eyes, "you've got to see a doctor."

I tried to explain how I felt to the doctor. "The nerve endings of my body feel as if they are hanging outside. I can't even take a shower, the water hitting me feels like hundreds of tiny needles. I can't sleep anymore. The most rest I get is a catnap of five minutes."

The doctor tried heavy medication to end my acute spells of dizziness. The medication caused my kidneys to fail temporarily. He prescribed tranquilizers for my nerves. Instead of calming me down, I became agitated . . . when the dosage was increased, it made me worse.

I tried constantly to reach God in prayer, but to no avail. I was mystified. I had prayed for thousands of people and they were healed without a problem, but now I was sick and God was silent.

"You're young, only twenty-nine years," the doctor said sternly, "too young to be having serious problems with nerves."

He was right. Yet, I had them. Problems loomed completely out of proportion to their actual size. It seemed as if whatever little control I had over myself might snap any minute, and I'd be floating in an emotional stream unable to return. What if that happened? What would I do then?

Being a strong-willed person, I fought to retain my sanity,

but the harder I fought the more tense I became. It seemed like an endless cycle that I was helpless to stop.

The doctor placed me on a special cream and milk diet, and for more than a month I stayed home while Tammy did the children's show and others did the "700 Club." I was crying out to God, "You've got to help me, Lord. You've got to show me the way out of this."

And, little-by-little, He did.

One day while I was still at home I listened to Dr. Claire Weekes from Australia being interviewed on TV. I thought she was talking about me because she described perfectly the situation I had been going through. I was immediately comforted because I had thought I was the only person alive with these horrible symptoms.

"When you find yourself getting tense," she explained, "don't fight to keep calm. Simply accept your condition and imagine you are floating on water or a fluffy cloud."

Immediately I could see the parallel of what Dr. Weekes was saying with the scriptures. Psalm 37:5 declares "commit thy way unto the Lord," and when you commit something you give it up. You don't fight. Then, I noticed Deuteronomy 33:27 . . . "the eternal God is thy refuge, and underneath are the everlasting arms." Instead of floating on water or a cloud, I began picturing myself floating in the arms of the Lord.

Later, I purchased a copy of her book, *Hope and Help for your Nerves,* and I could see that millions of people were responding to their problems as I had. I began to release the burden of CBN's finances to the Lord, and gradually I felt a gentle easing in my spirit.

I was leafing through the pages of my Bible one day when I ran across some notes on the prophecy given over Tammy and me back at Minneapolis Evangelistic Auditorium. Reading down the page, my eyes came to the sentence: "The Lord wants you to get plenty of rest, if you don't, the devil will use it against you."

You!

The word seemed to glare back at me from the page. Tears filled my eyes as I recalled that moment eight years before when the Lord had given me that warning, a warning I had failed to heed.

I had violated one of God's fixed laws. I had misused my body. I had robbed it for years by not eating or resting properly. And the consequence of breaking that law was predictable—breakdown!

I loved the work on Christian television so much I practically spent my every waking moment there. That's why I kept saying, "Lord, I don't understand all this. I'm a happy person. I love my work." But the Lord showed me a mental picture of Jim Bakker constantly on the run, always grabbing a sandwich. I was disobedient and my happiness ill-founded.

As my body slowly began to mend, Tammy and I decided to take a trip to her home. After our stay in International Falls, we traveled into Canada to visit some friends. When we arrived unannounced at a minister-friend's home, she looked a little surprised.

"Jim," she said, "I've had you on my heart for some time. The Lord has been speaking to me about you."

"Really?" I replied.

"Yes," she nodded. "You're not getting enough diversion in your life. Jim, you need to do something besides praying and preaching all the time. You need recreation and exercise, too."

She was right . . . and God, in His love, had brought me all the way to Canada to hear the truth. My life was entirely wrapped up in Christian television. I had no hobby, no other pursuit.

Back at our beautiful home on the lake in Virginia, the Lord sent me outside saying: *Go fishing*. As I sat beside the water watching the ripples widen around the float on my fishing line, I saw why Jesus had spent so much time with his disciples beside the sea. There is something tranquil and peaceful about the water.

And I began mowing my own lawn. Kids would ride up on their bikes and ask to mow the lawn. "Sorry," I'd say with a grin, "this is saving my life."

On the weekend before I was scheduled to go back to work, I was driving to the grocery store when the Lord spoke to me as I stopped at a red light. *Jim,* He said, *you're trying to do the work of God. You're trying to play God.*

I recognized what the Lord was saying. For example, people would often call the station after I had interviewed a guest on the program. "Do you know who you just had on the show?" they would ask.

"Yes, but what do you mean?" I would answer back.

"He's in false doctrine," came the standard reply.

After I had gotten a rash of these phone calls, I began to fret and fume about the guests who appeared on the show. The phone calls really worried me. Who was right? Who was wrong? Pretty soon, I couldn't tell which end was up.

The Lord spoke again. *Jim, I'll judge these people. Your job is to just love them.*

"That's a deal, God," I announced firmly while horns honked behind me trying to bring my attention to the green light.

It was as if a load of bricks had been lifted from my shoulders when I realized I didn't have to figure out who was right or wrong in all the endless disputes over doctrine. All God wanted Jim Bakker to do was release the worry and anxiety, so that He could love these people through me. I had preached that, yet, when it came right down to it, I wasn't practicing my own preaching.

While I was gradually recovering, Tammy went to the doctor for a physical, and he, surprisingly, suggested she get pregnant for my sake. She asked him to phone me. "Jim," he said, "I think it would help you if you and Tammy had a baby. You need still more to get your mind off your work and on something else."

We had never tried to have children before, because I

thought they didn't fit into our busy schedule. We both loved children, but with our jam-packed activities, we wouldn't, I was afraid, have time for ones of our own. I had seen too many children of busy parents hungry for love and affection and not getting it.

When Tammy came home, we sat down and talked again. Finally, I said, "Okay honey, as long as you're all right physically, we'll try to have a baby. I believe God will have me ready to start being a father in time."

Less than five feet tall and expanding like a fragile balloon, Tammy got incessant kidding from the production crew. Dale Hill jokingly renamed the program, the "Jim and *Tummy* Show."

Tammy Sue Bakker was born in March 1970, and the Lord restored me completely. I was ready to move on with God.

Right from the start, Tammy Sue seemed to belong to our viewers as much as she did to Tammy and me. Our viewers' reaction to her birth was unreal. Hospital officials said Tammy received more telephone calls and cards than anyone in the history of Maryview Hospital. Tammy Sue received so many gifts of clothing that we didn't have to buy her anything but diapers the first two years of her life. We gave the rest of the clothing away to Tidewater orphanages.

I had been up almost all night waiting for Tammy Sue's birth, so the next day, when I arrived at the studio, I was simultaneously exhilarated and exhausted. I was partially dazed that evening when I went through the motions of doing the show. "Tammy Sue Bakker was born today," I announced proudly, "and she's really quite a little girl. She weighs nineteen-and-a-half pounds and is six-and-a-half inches long!" That one elicited a few perplexed calls after the show.

Before the baby's birth Tammy had been an unusually healthy person. Thus she had never used any of the drugs that many Americans take regularly. That Sunday morning she was already in labor when I took her to the hospital around ten o'clock, but once she had been given pain-killing shots, her contractions slowed down and more than twelve hours elapsed before Tammy Sue was born.

I knew Tammy had experienced a long and painful labor, but I didn't realize how serious it had been until the following Tuesday. Walking into her room, I noticed that she had been crying and her eyes were swollen and red. She seemed to be in a daze.

"Honey," I said excitedly, "aren't you happy about our little baby girl?"

She gave me a strange stare and began to cry again. "What baby are you talking about?" she asked, slurring almost every word.

"The baby you had on Monday," I answered, trying to get her to stop crying. "Our baby is the one I'm talking about."

"I don't know," she said turning her head to the side as tears began to stain her starched white pillow.

Walking out to the nurse's station, I spoke to the head nurse, "What's wrong with my wife?"

She shook her head. "I'm not quite sure," she responded, "but last night we had to have someone with her constantly. She thought there were huge spiders crawling over the drapes, and she tried to get out of bed to kill them. Then she thought there were mice underneath the bed."

"I don't believe it."

Taking off her glasses she looked at me seriously. "It's true," she said, pointing to a nurse's report. "It seems almost like a bad drug trip to me, or hallucinations."

"But how could something like that happen?" I asked. "She's a perfectly healthy person in here just to have a baby."

"It could be some adverse reaction to the drugs," the nurse suggested, "and in time it should work itself out."

And that's the way I left it. With God's help and Tammy's

boundless energy, I knew she would be back to normal soon. To help out, I called her Grandma Fairchild and asked her to come help with Tammy Sue.

Soon after Tammy was released from the hospital, she went back to work. But as the weeks began passing, I noticed that Tammy was wearing thin under the strain of the daily show, even though she tried to act like her old self.

At times I would find her alone at home crying, for what seemed like no reason at all. Even worse, it seemed we were growing apart for the first time in our marriage. We could no longer communicate with one another.

She gradually stopped appearing on the "700 Club" and at other special occasions, and withdrew into herself. Tammy seemed to be trying to pull a protective covering over herself, like a turtle pulling back into its shell when in danger.

After several months I realized it couldn't go on like this. We had always been partners in the ministry and now we were growing distant. I couldn't survive that way for long.

"Tammy, something's wrong," I remarked one night while getting ready for bed. "You don't laugh any more. You don't smile. I can't take you places any longer because you start crying at the least thing. What's the matter? Don't you love me any more?"

She looked up from her reading in bed. "Jim, you know I love you," she answered flatly. "There's nothing wrong . . . absolutely nothing."

"But you've changed since you had the baby," tears began to trickle down my cheeks. "Our life together isn't what it used to be."

"There's nothing wrong," she clicked off her bed lamp and pulled the covers up with a note of finality. "There's nothing wrong, Jim."

But there *was* something wrong. The worst of it was that Tammy couldn't even admit to herself that a problem existed. As I daily drove to and from the studio, I cried out for God's help to restore Tammy and heal our relationship. If He didn't help, all might be lost . . . even our marriage.

I suspected Tammy's problems were being caused largely by her body's reaction to the drugs, but I didn't suspect the real depth of those problems. The medication had jangled her emotions in such a way she couldn't feel the presence of the Lord anymore. She was even doubting her own salvation.

Almost five months after Tammy Sue's birth, Tammy finally opened up. "Jim," she said walking into the den where I was looking over my sermon notes for an upcoming revival, "I need to talk."

"Sure honey," I said brushing a lock of hair from my eyes. "What's up?"

She looked more serious than I had ever seen her. "I think I need a psychiatrist."

"A psychiatrist?"

"Yes," she answered, nervously twisting a string on her dress. "I just can't seem to lick this problem myself. I need some help."

"But a psychiatrist?" I asked.

All night I twisted and squirmed in bed thinking of all the ramifications of Tammy's possible visit to a psychiatrist. I felt like such a failure. For months my own wife had been in need of help, help I hadn't been able to give.

Finally I got out of bed and walked to the sliding glass doors overlooking the lake. A full moon stood high in the night sky, its soft light danced on the rippling water below. "God," I said, pressing my face against the glass, "I don't know what to do any more. I give up . . . this problem is too much for me."

That morning, I left for the studio early.

Tammy arose later and began thumbing through the phone book looking for a psychiatrist's telephone number. Picking up the phone, she began dialing.

85

Suddenly the Lord spoke: *Tammy, let me be your psychiatrist.*

Tammy fell on her knees beside the couch and began weeping. "Lord . . . Lord," she cried out, "I thought you had left me. Oh, God."

Tammy, doesn't my word say that I will never forsake you or leave you?

"Yes," she sobbed.

Will I not keep them that the Father has given me? He questioned.

"Yes, Lord," Tammy cried.

Tammy phoned me. "The Lord is still with me," she said through the tears. From that point on, she began walking more by faith and less by feelings. Little by little, God began to restore Tammy.

Believers in the Tidewater area had continually prayed for a move of the Holy Spirit there. Finally someone suggested, "If we want the Spirit to move, why don't we have a meeting and call it a Holy Ghost rally?"

Local churches cooperated, and leased the Virginia Beach Dome for a week's meetings. I was among those who were asked to lead the meetings. One night I was praying for the sick. The Dome was packed to capacity and people streamed forward for ministry.

I noticed a woman standing beside me on the stage. Turning to Henry Harrison who was ministering with me, I asked, "What is that woman doing on the stage?"

"She's just walked out of a wheelchair," Henry answered softly.

The woman's healing almost broke up the whole meeting. She had been paralyzed for some twenty years, since a freak automobile accident. Her healing convinced me as never before that God is entirely in charge of miracles. The move of God's Spirit which people had prayed for was happening. Hundreds were touched and healed.

Before the meeting ended that night, Buddy Smith, a man in his early thirties, was brought forward for prayer. Afflicted with multiple sclerosis, Buddy had not walked in years and had to be carried. He had lost control of his bodily functions and had to wear diapers. I placed my hand on Buddy's head and his friends laid hands on him, and we all united in prayer for about five minutes.

Then they picked him up and carried him out to the car. They drove back across the James River Bridge, and by the time their car hit the streets of Newport News, Buddy Smith was healed.

When they pulled up in front of Buddy's house, he leaped out of the car and went running up and down the street. He rang the doorbells of his neighbors' homes and they all had a victory parade down the middle of the street at three o'clock in the morning.

Buddy's family owned a chain of dry cleaning stores in Newport News, and he went back to work for the first time in years. He sometimes worked sixty hours a week testifying in the store and sharing Christ with everyone he came in contact with. Weeks later his physical therapist called me. ''This is the greatest miracle I've ever heard about,'' she exclaimed.

Later that same week, I was hosting the ''700 Club'' and couldn't attend the night Tammy was scheduled to sing at the Dome. For almost a year she had turned down repeated requests to sing, but finally she had been convinced to step out in faith to begin ministering again.

Tammy was pretty nervous that night when Roger and Linda Wilson arrived to drive her to the Dome. But as she began singing ''The King Is Coming,'' the crowd of some two thousand stood with hands raised in praise to the King—Jesus.

After she sang, the preacher came to the rostrum, but he couldn't preach. ''Tammy,'' he said happily, ''the Lord wants to use you tonight. Would you come back to the platform?''

With microphone in hand she sang and spoke for the glory

of God. Over a hundred people came forward to receive Christ. It was another act of God's Spirit in a week filled with the Lord's special presence.

Once the service ended, a woman approached Tammy. "I wanted to tell you," she confided, "While you were singing tonight, I saw lights like Fourth of July sparklers showering all over you from the top of your head."

Tears streamed down Tammy's face. "God was doing something to you right there in front of everybody," the woman added.

That was confirmation to us both that God had completely restored her. We had been through seemingly endless valleys, but God had been faithful to bring us back out into the light and we believed that our experiences would one day help others who faced similar struggles.

A *Jim at an early age sitting between his parents. Behind them (from the left) are his brothers, Norman and Bob, and his sister, Donna.*

B *Here's little Jim holding big brother Norman's hand while Donna looks on. Muskegon, 1942.*

C *Dad snapped this one on Donna's graduation day. Norman's on the left, Jim on the right. This is while they lived in the orange house.*

D

E

D *Jim and Tammy in the early days of their marriage.*
E *The Reverend and Mrs. LeRoy Howe, with Jim and Tammy, "breaking the record" with a large crowd at the Warwick Assembly of God, Newport News, Virginia.*

Photos by Philip D. Egert

F *Tammy with her Cordovox which she played in their revivals (February, 1964).*

G *Jim and Tammy with their puppets.*

H *The famous first Halloween party on the "Jim and Tammy Show" at CBN.*

I

J

Photos by Philip D. Egert

I   *The "Jim and Tammy Show"—on the air.*
J   *A typical scene from one of the early "700 Club" telethons; Jim busily engaged on the phone.*

K

L

Photo by Philip D. Egert

K *Tammy Bakker, Jan Crouch, and little Tammy Sue removing tile from the floor of the new facilities for Channel 46, Irvine, California.*

L *The Bakker family (Jim, Tammy holding Jamie Charles, and Tammy Sue) with Henry Harrison at a recent telethon in Charlotte.*

Photos by Philip D. Egert

M   *On the "PTL Club" set in Charlotte. From the left: Jim Moss, Larry Hall, A.T. Lawing, Bill Flint (the four, with Jim, comprise the board of directors), Judy Chavez, and Jim.*

N   *Dan Malachuk, president of Logos International, and Jim agreeing to do a book about Jim's life. Henry Harrison looks on.*

O

P

Photos by Philip D. Egert

O *October 20, 1975, Jim and Tammy break ground for the PTL Heritage Center in Charlotte.*

P *December, 1975, a giant plastic tent allows construction to continue at Heritage Center.*

Q

R

Photos by Philip D. Egert

Q *On February 20, 1976, workmen raised the first stage of the steeple at Heritage Center.*

R *The night of the bomb threat, March 3, 1976, at Heritage Center. From the left, Ann Fenton, Henry Harrison, Jim, Joyce Scarborough, Phil Fenton (security guard), and Richard Scarborough.*

9

"In Everything Give Thanks"

From my days in Minneapolis sitting under the teaching of the Olsons, I had known that God promises believers in Romans 8:28 that "all things work together for good." But my understanding of it was considerably increased one night, while hosting the "700 Club." Merlin Carothers—author of the highly successful books on praise—was my guest.

"If you believe that all things work together for good," Carothers said, "then for everything that comes along you can give God thanks. According to I Thessalonians 5:18, that's God's will for our lives."

"Are you saying we should give thanks for absolutely *everything* that happens in our lives?"

"Yes," he smiled. "We should thank God because it's all working together for good, our good!"

"Would you agree that the quickest way out of the valley of despondency is by means of praise?" I inquired.

He nodded his head. "That's right, Jim. As long as we

grumble and complain we're going to have problems. Praise is really the way out of the valley or any other situation for that matter.''

Shortly after that broadcast, Tammy and I were on our way to Atlanta for a telethon. But that morning we developed car trouble and I had to drive over to a garage that specialized in front end work. The car was quickly examined and the manager reported, ''You have bad shocks. We'll have to replace them.''

''Fine,'' I said, ''go ahead and do it.''

The Lord had been dealing with me for months about praising Him so, as I walked into the waiting room of the shop, I began praising the Lord for this delay and asking Him to bless the manager and his mechanics. Carothers had said if you are ever delayed to begin praying for others and praising God.

Moments later the manager was back again. ''I'm sorry sir,'' he said wiping his hands on a greasy rag, ''but your ball joints have gone out, too. They need replacing.''

''Go ahead,'' I said, continuing to praise the Lord all the while.

Shortly he came back a third time. ''I don't understand it,'' he said apologetically, ''but your tie rods are worn out. We'll have to replace them also.''

''Fine, go ahead,'' I said. But for the next several hours, the manager kept coming back with part after part that had to be replaced. It was taking so long that Tammy decided to join me and together we began praising the Lord and praying for the men in the garage.

About $200 in repairs and hours later, we finally got on the road and then it began to rain. I started to complain a bit, but my secretary, Linda Cochran, who was making the trip with us, spoke up, ''Why don't you praise the Lord for the rain, Jim?''

I couldn't stand it. I had been preaching praise to everybody, and now I was getting my own sermon back in my face!

So we all joined in obediently thanking the Lord for the

rain—which was a little difficult since it had been raining off and on for ten days. But in ten minutes the rain stopped!

That night I was supposed to have met some people in Charlotte, but I missed the appointment due to the delay. They called later at our motel to report that they had gone to a healing service in lieu of our meeting, and one had received a spinal healing while another had been baptized with the Holy Spirit. So already I could see a purpose for our delay. God knew best.

The next day, we drove into a service station in Atlanta looking for the Days Inn motel. Just as our car pulled across the black hose that rang the bell and the station manager came to the door, strange squeeking noises began coming from the automobile.

The burly manager walked to the car and began pushing up and down on the fender. "It sounds like your shocks are gone," he pronounced matter-of-factly.

"That's impossible," I said wearily. "I just had new ones put on yesterday morning."

"Let's put it on the grease rack and see," he suggested.

I drove into the service bay, and the Cadillac was quickly elevated into full view. Tammy and I had taken seats in the waiting room when the manager walked in saying, "We'll take care of it. The folks who did your work forgot to put any grease fittings on."

"What's the charge?" I asked.

"Oh no," he said shaking his head, "there's no charge."

We got instructions from the service station manager, and found our way over to the motel where I dressed hurriedly for the telethon.

After I left for the studio, Tammy received a phone call. "I'm the wife of the service station man you folks met today," the woman explained. "My husband told me about you driving in, and I'm calling to ask you to pray for him. I'm a Christian, but he's not."

"I've already been praying for him," Tammy answered.

"While I was waiting in the station today, the Lord told me to pray for him and the other men."

The woman began crying. "I know the Lord's going to save him," she said. "We watched you folks on television last night, and out of all the hundreds of gas stations in Atlanta, you drove into his today. It's already a miracle of God."

Indeed, before the night was out, the woman called Tammy back to report that her husband had come to Christ.

The next day Tammy and I were to make a public appearance at an Atlanta shopping center in conjunction with our children's show. When we arrived several hundred people were waiting, but our puppet stage had gotten lost.

People, from grandmas to small children, were tugging at my coat sleeve and grabbing at me and, on top of all that, it was sticky hot and started to rain.. Everything was going wrong and I began to panic.

Sweat dripped off my forehead and down my face. Finally I had to remove my coat. I could feel my wilted shirt sticking to my back as I tried to survey the situation.

The Scripture, "In everything give thanks," came to me. "How can I thank You for this situation, Lord?" I asked bleakly.

Try anyway, the Lord seemed to be saying to me.

I wiped my forehead. "Well, praise the Lord," I muttered. "Father, I ask You to do something with this situation. But Lord, whether You do or not, I praise You anyway. Glory to Your name." I began to feel better, even though nothing had actually changed.

People all around me were offering suggestions as to what I could do. "There's an auditorium in the basement of the shopping center," someone finally said.

I walked into the mall to check on the auditorium, and the whole crowd of several hundred people followed me in. I quickly located the auditorium. About the same time, the truck drove up with all our sound equipment and stage . . . and in short order,

Susie Moppet and her family were on stage to the delight of everybody.

After the program people began walking up to ask me to pray with them. Quickly, a healing line formed in the basement as the Spirit of God began touching people's sick and diseased bodies.

That night when I arrived back at the station for the second night of the telethon, calls were already coming in from people who had been healed in the basement of that shopping center. It finally dawned on me how great a miracle God had done. He had guided us into that basement so that we could pray for the sick. That wouldn't have been allowed in the shopping center's parking lot or mall.

Later on our way back home, I spoke in a Presbyterian church in Charlotte and told the wonderful story of praise. God's blessing on our trip to Atlanta excellently illustrated the value of praise.

Afterward a man and his wife walked up to shake my hand. "Jim," the man said, "the Lord spoke to us while you were speaking, and we'd like to buy you a new wardrobe. Can you go with us tomorrow to take care of that?"

"Yes sir, I certainly can," I answered.

And sure enough, they drove me around the next day in their custom-built Lincoln, and purchased an entire wardrobe of clothes for me—shirts, shoes, coats, socks, pants—the "works."

That praise story brought blessing after blessing to all who heard it, including me! In every situation, the child of God can praise and thank Him when he knows it's all working together for his good.

10

Death at
Five or Fifty

Around 150 kids showed up at the studio each day we did the "Jim and Tammy Show." It was difficult to get to know many of them personally. But six-year-old Susie Ferrer stood out. Maybe it was her wide brown eyes or soft cameo face. I don't know exactly what it was, but she was special.

Her mother was a volunteer at CBN, so naturally Susie was frequently at the station participating in the show. She especially enjoyed our Halloween program when we would dig out a large pumpkin with all the kids' messy help.

Unknown to us, Susie was a hemophiliac, a "bleeder." She was a healthy-looking child, so we had no cause to suspect something was wrong, until a friend of Mrs. Ferrer's called. "Susie died in her daddy's arms while being rushed to the hospital," she said.

Tammy and I were crushed by the news. It didn't seem possible that the bright and lively child we had known was dead.

"Jim," Mrs. Ferrer's friend said, "Susie's mother wants you to preach the funeral and she also wants Tammy to sing."

"Oh, no," I protested, "we couldn't do that."

My refusal touched a sensitive chord with this woman, and she began crying over the phone. "Listen Jim," she stammered through the tears, "Susie loved you and Tammy. You were her favorites. Please, couldn't you do this for her?"

I promised to call Mrs. Ferrer with my answer, and for the next few hours Tammy and I talked and cried. It wasn't that I didn't want to handle the funeral, but that I was afraid I'd get there and be unable to preach. We prayed together and I submitted the decision to the Lord.

"Father," I prayed, "I don't really know if I can do it. But, Lord, I submit to Your will."

Somehow, deep inside, I felt a gentle peace coming over me and I knew God's answer was "yes." I telephoned Mrs. Ferrer to tell her.

I began to prepare a message for the funeral. Yet, I could hardly think about it without breaking down in tears. Tammy was having the same trouble with her songs. She couldn't practice for crying.

"Honey," I suggested finally, "I think it might help us both if we go down to the funeral home and see Susie."

Tammy wasn't quite as sure. But she consented shortly and we drove downtown. Walking into the funeral home, the attendant led us back to what he called a "slumber room." We looked down at the body of the little girl in the casket.

"You know, Jim," Tammy remarked, clutching my hand tightly, "that's not Susie. The sparkle isn't there any more."

"You're right," I answered, "Susie's not here. She's with Jesus."

And as we walked from the funeral home into the warmth of the afternoon sun, the Lord reminded me of the promise in

Revelation 21:4 ". . . and there shall be no more death, neither sorrow, nor crying, neither shall there be any more pain: for the former things are passed away."

The Lord seemed to be saying: *That's where Susie is. Where there is no sorrow, crying or pain. She's with Me.*

I knew then that I was to preach a victorious message on dying as a Christian. Death was not defeat, but victory. And, indeed, God gave me great liberty at the funeral to speak about little Susie's promotion to be with God.

The congregation responded warmly to this note of victory and broke out in spontaneous praises to the Lord. Tammy added the crowning touch to the occasion by singing Susie's favorite songs, "Love Lifted Me" and "Jesus Loves Me."

All through the funeral I noticed the calmness and composure of Susie's parents. Afterward they approached me. "Jim, you have completely captured all the things Susie was interested in," Mrs. Ferrer remarked. "I know the Lord gave you that message."

"I have been greatly blessed by seeing your composure in the face of losing Susie," I said. "I'll never forget it and I'm sure Tammy won't."

"We've learned a secret through this," Mr. Ferrer spoke up. "We're not operating in our own strength. We're operating in God's."

We dedicated the next day's "Jim and Tammy Show" to Susie's memory. At the beginning of the program, a picture of Susie was flashed on the screen and we announced that she had gone home to be with Jesus. It was a unique opportunity to explain about dying to the kids.

Seating the youngsters around the set's familiar tree stump, I began telling the story of Noah and the ark. "Noah was prepared for the flood," I said, "but everybody else wasn't. Susie Ferrer was prepared for death, but very few people are."

The children sat attentively while I explained. "It doesn't

make any difference what your age—whether you're five or fifty—you must be prepared to meet Jesus at any time."

"Are you ready?" I asked as the camera began to focus on the children's faces. "Are you ready?"

Even before the show left the air, calls began lighting up the CBN switchboard as viewers, young and old, began responding to the program. Calls continued pouring in while the "700 Club" was being broadcast. People were receiving Jesus as their Savior following that simple kid's show with the story of Noah and the ark.

We actually had to call in extra helpers as the calls overloaded the switchboard. More than a thousand decisions were made for Christ, and in death, Susie Ferrer was winning people to the Lord.

Several weeks later a tape of that same "Jim and Tammy Show" was telecast "by mistake." I was home cleaning out the garage when Tammy called me to the phone. "It's the station calling," she shouted.

I hurried to the house wondering what the call was about. "You've got to come in," the caller urged, "the phones are ringing off the hook. That program was run by mistake. Get here as fast as you can."

Once at the station, we both handled as many calls as we could before making an on-the-air appeal for some CBN counselors to come in to help. Another five hundred decisions were made that day just because a technician supposedly made a mistake and ran the show.

The importance of being prepared to meet Jesus at any age was again brought home to me months later when my oldest brother, Bob, was dying. Hospitalized in a veteran's center in Tucson, Arizona, Bob's life of rebellion and independence was slowly coming to an end.

Bob was the brother I had never really known. He was

more than fifteen years older than I, and had left home before I was old enough to know him. As a teenager, he had been unusually rebellious. He had stolen daddy's car on one occasion and wound up in a Texas jail. Later Bob accepted Christ and finished Central Bible College in Springfield, Missouri.

But after pastoring a little pioneer church in the Ozarks for several years, confusion again entered Bob's life. Somehow he got mixed up with erroneous doctrine and ultimately left his wife and children on the advice of a false prophet. Within a matter of months after that, Bob had turned his back on the Lord.

Any time there was prayer in a service for a lost relative, I always stood up for Bob. I continually prayed that God would redeem him. Occasionally, when I would lead an altar call in a revival and see people streaming forward to accept Christ, my eyes would fill with tears as I thought about the lost sheep of the Bakker family, Bob.

A handsome, personable guy, Bob was successfully running a nightclub in Arizona when kidney disease struck him down. Since he always had a flair for exaggerating situations, I wasn't even sure if the information I had on his illness was correct. I called the hospital long distance and spoke to a nurse on his floor.

"Is it true my brother is dying?" I asked in the hopes of getting some information without running into any red tape.

"I'm sorry sir, we don't give out that information over the phone."

After considerable effort, I finally convinced her that I really was Bob's brother and also a clergyman. "Yes, it's true," she finally admitted. "He has a rare kidney disease, and at best he has only a few weeks to live."

Calling my sister Donna on the phone, we both decided to fly out to Arizona and see Bob. When we walked into his room, I was surprised. His appearance was, of course, drastically changed from the last time I had seen him, but his attitude was unexpectedly good.

He welcomed us warmly. "Say Jim," he asked, "read I Corinthians 13 for me." Handing me a copy of the Living Bible he remarked, "I want to hear the love chapter."

"Where did you get that?" I said reaching for the Bible.

"Our cousin, Margie Klages, was here a few weeks ago," he answered smiling, "and she left it with me."

As we talked, I learned that God had led Margie, a dedicated Christian, to Bob's bedside. Through her tender love and compassion, Bob had come back to Christ.

Donna and I were greatly relieved by this tremendous change in Bob. His body was gaunt and rail thin, and his skin had turned a dull yellowish color. Most of his hair has fallen out, so that Bob looked to be over sixty years old. In reality, he was just in his late forties.

Silently, I praised God that Bob could still walk and talk although somewhat falteringly . . . and for the next several days that's all we did.

The brother I had never really known walked arm-in-arm over the manicured grounds of that hospital with me. Sitting in lawn chairs one afternoon we gazed at the stark mountains in the distance. I turned to him, "Bob I love you." It was the first time in my life I had said it to him.

Bob was able to express his love for the first time as well. Tears fell from my eyes as I sat talking with my wandering brother who had come home. Bob told me tearfully how he had explained to each of his six children that he was going to die. "And then," he said emotionally, "I gave them each a memento from among my things."

My parents arrived while Donna and I were still there and we borrowed their car for a trip to Phoenix. I had heard there was a Christian television station there carrying the "Jim and Tammy Show," and I wanted to pay the station a visit.

When we walked into the general manager's office, the

man's face completely turned white. "Is there anything the matter?" I asked.

Tears came to his eyes. "I can't believe you're here," he said, wiping his eyes with his handkerchief.

"I'm sorry," I remarked, "but I don't quite understand what's going on."

"I've heard you're the greatest fund raiser in Christian television," he said, "and for you to walk into my office today—I can't believe it. We closed out our telethon last night without having reached half of our goal. We're going bankrupt. There's no way we can make it. Is there any way you can stay and help?" he asked pleadingly.

"I'll call Pat Robertson and see if I can stay a few days," I promised. Pat agreed to let me stay three days, Monday through Wednesday.

Tammy flew out to help with the expanded telethon, and by Wednesday night, the station's goal had been fully reached. God's plan amazed me. He had used a visit to Bob to get me to Arizona. Then a spur-of-the-moment "whim" had brought me to Phoenix. In retrospect I realized it was the Holy Spirit's leading, entirely.

Before returning to Portsmouth, we decided to visit John Shamel in a Phoenix suburb. It was John who had lifted Jimmy Summerfield's body from beneath my father's car that cold, snowy night years before in Muskegon.

Our visit with the Shamels ran into Sunday and I decided, uncharacteristically, to stay home while everybody else left for church. "I feel like the Lord wants to speak to me alone," I had explained to Tammy.

After reading and praying for a while, I walked from John's house to the foothills of a mountain range that rose silently toward the sky. The sun turned bright amber as I walked among the desert cacti before reaching some barren, iron-colored rocks.

The minute my feet touched the rocks I sensed the nearness

of God's presence. That presence seemed to draw closer as I climbed up the mountain . . . and I began talking to the Lord.

A solitary bird hovered overhead riding the air currents on its outstretched wings when I reached a spot near the top and looked back down at the Shamels' house. It looked no larger than a matchbox in the distance.

A question had been troubling me for some time. Tens of thousands of denominational people had received the Baptism with the Holy Spirit. The question was whether these people should remain in their churches or leave them to join Pentecostal or charismatic churches or fellowships. So I asked the Lord this question.

Come with me, He said. As we walked over the top of a nearby knoll, I saw some old fences standing in a line. *Do you see these fences?*

"Yes, Lord," I responded.

These fences are like the denominations, He said. *They are barriers between My people which I did not build,* He said, *but I don't want you tearing them down. I have ways around them.*

As we walked a little further, a gate appeared. *See?* He asked. *I have a way around the barriers that you know not of.*

I had my answer. I was not to work in any way to tear down the denominational churches. I was to work with them. It would be important to my life and ministry.

Then the Lord seemed to be drawing my attention to a rugged mountain standing in the distance. *That's a big mountain, isn't it?*

"Yes, it is," I answered.

That mountain is only made up of rocks and stones, the Lord pointed out. *Sometimes people see a great man of God lifted up and they fail to see the rocks and stones which are the souls he's touching for Christ. But they are the only reason he is allowed to be lifted up . . . for these souls.*

The Lord's words bore heavily upon me as I reflected on

the instantaneous recognition that television brings—in some cases lifting up people who aren't ready to handle what comes with that adulation.

That morning, as the Lord talked, I wrote down what He said. It filled seven full pages. I sensed that a change was coming into my life, maybe one that would completely uproot us.

At one point, a tiny bee began buzzing, and I momentarily looked to see where the sound was coming from. *See?* the Lord chided, *even the slightest thing distracts you from the sound of My voice. You must come away to talk with Me more often.*

In the days and months that lay ahead, circumstances would often lead me to go aside to pray and listen to God speak.

11

Sheet
of Blackness

I came back home from my experience on the mountain with a gnawing unsettled feeling inside. It was hard to explain.

Outwardly things couldn't have been better.

I had a nice income, national exposure for my ministry on television, a beautiful house on a lake and a host of lovely friends in a community where we had finally put down some roots for the first time in eleven years.

But this unsettled feeling continued to trouble me. At first I thought it was the constant pressure of my schedule at CBN. Frequently I traveled around the country working in telethons with Pat as the ministry expanded into major new outlets.

Three nights a week, I hosted the "700 Club" and five times a week we did the "Jim and Tammy Show." The children's program was at the peak of its popularity, as we found out when we offered a little ring and certificate to members of our Friendship Club. Thousands of requests poured into the station.

Yet at night, Tammy and I would lay awake for long hours talking about our strange feelings and wondering what God was up to.

And for several months, the whole situation amounted to nothing more than that: talk.

But the eighth day of November 1972 arrived, and as I dressed for work, the Lord spoke to me, *I want you to resign your job at CBN today.*

I didn't like the idea much. I had an expensive house to continue paying for, and without a regular paycheck, I would quickly lose it as well as my automobile.

"God, I'll make a deal with You," I said, foolishly trying to bargain with the Lord. "You sell my house, and then I'll resign the job."

No, he answered, *you must resign first, and then I will sell your house.*

Perplexed, I walked into the kitchen where Tammy was washing the breakfast dishes. Sunlight streamed through the window catching the brightness of her blonde hair as she looked up from the dishes.

"Honey," I said sitting down at the table, "the Lord said today's the day."

"The day for what?"

"Today's the day the Lord said I'm to resign from CBN," my voice quavered.

Tears trickled down her cheeks as she walked over to me. I put my arms around her waist and held her tightly for a few minutes. "Tammy, what shall I do?"

She rubbed the back of my neck lightly, "You've got to do what the Lord has told you."

I knew that Tammy was with me. For all our married life we had worked together as a team . . . her support had always been essential and now with this crucial decision we were in agreement. Years ago I had learned that a man and wife could hardly function

106

unless they are agreed (Amos 3:3). With Tammy's support, I could drive to the studios with more confidence in the face of this major upheaval in our lives

Within thirty minutes, I was seated in Pat Robertson's office. We chatted briefly and then I spoke up. "Pat," I began falteringly, "God has told me to leave CBN."

Pat seemed amazingly calm. "If God has told you, I can't argue with that. In my heart, I don't want you to go. In fact, the board of directors has just voted you a salary increase."

I tried to smile, but it was difficult for me. "I have to leave. I don't know what God has in mind for us, but I know He's speaking to me to resign."

"You've got to do what God says. As much as I'd like to, I can't hold onto you. But I want you to know that you always have a place here."

I tried to tell Pat how much I appreciated his friendship, but somehow I couldn't seem to find the words. Pat Robertson had made a profound impression on my life during the seven years we had worked together. We came from very different backgrounds, but God had molded us into a good team at CBN. I would be forever grateful for what Pat had done for Tammy and me.

That night, Tammy and I sat watching a taped rerun of the "Jim and Tammy Show" and later one of the "700 Club." It seemed as if seven years of our lives was wrapped up in those programs as we watched through tear-stained eyes.

We kept thinking that God had surely made a mistake this time. Could He really mean for us to leave Christian television? Wasn't this the ministry He had placed us in? Maybe He didn't mean for us to leave Christian television, but He did mean for us to resign . . . and in obedience we had.

Farewell activities were planned, and Nancy Harman, who had been a frequent guest on the "700 Club," came to sing. The program was televised live over Channel 27. Everybody seemed to be in tears that night, especially Tammy and I. They asked Tammy to sing one more song, and I closed by reading I Corinthians 13 in the Living Bible, the same Scripture Bob had asked me to read when I visited him in the hospital. Then Pat presented us with a silver tea service—"For your seven years of faithful service to the Christian Broadcasting Network," he said.

And with that, we bade farewell to our friends.

That night I walked out of the building ahead of Tammy. As I did, I remembered when that studio had been put up. I had watched all the steel and bricks go into place. That building was a part of me. Yet, in one moment, it became a part of my past. I was an outsider now.

When I reached the parking lot—where seven years before we had felt God's hand moving us to join CBN—I wondered aloud: "Well, here I am, foot-loose and fancy free. What am I going to do now?"

I have called you away, not to divide, but to multiply. God could not have comforted my troubled heart more perfectly. His words reassured me that He was in charge.

It was dark that night. No stars or moon were in sight. I looked into a sheet of blackness. The future was unknown— cloaked in that darkened sheet. Without a doubt, God would be my only support in whatever lay ahead.

12

"What's a Guasti?"

Several weeks passed after my resignation from CBN and our house on the lake hadn't sold. I had listed with a realtor and his sign was posted on the lawn, but there had been no takers yet.

The house payment would come due in a few days and I was getting desperate—desperate enough that I almost called the realtor and dropped the price $10,000 just to move the house off the market.

But one morning while I was shaving in the bathroom, the Lord suddenly spoke. *Get your house ready, I have someone coming to buy it today.*

I was so thrilled to be getting some direction I shouted "Hallelujah!" and almost cut my throat.

Tammy had been in the bedroom making up the bed, and she quickly stuck her head into the bathroom. "What's up?" she asked.

"The Lord just spoke to me and said to get the house cleaned," I answered excitedly. "He's going to sell it today."

Quickly, we began putting everything in order. I ran the vacuum cleaner and arranged the furniture while Tammy dusted and did some mopping.

That afternoon about three o'clock, the doorbell rang. There was a couple standing at the door. "I'm being transferred to this area from New Jersey, and we were out house hunting and got lost," the man explained. "Then I happened down your street and saw the 'for sale' sign on the lawn."

I winked at Tammy. The Lord had steered this couple to our house. "Come on in and look at the house," I said with a happy grin.

And it was almost as if the counterpart of Jim and Tammy Bakker had appeared at our door. The couple liked every feature we had added to the lakefront house. In fact, not only did they want to buy the house, but practically every stick of furniture in it, including a few of our appliances. Since we had no idea where we would be going and felt the Lord wanted us to be "mobile," we sold it all.

What they didn't purchase, a garage sale finished off a few weeks later. It was difficult to part with some things that had been with us since our married life began—but just as we had done back in 1961 when we left Minneapolis to go on the evangelistic field, we let go of the possessions knowing we were in God's will. Friends bought most of the stuff and we even disposed of Tammy Sue's larger toys. That was hard for her; she couldn't understand why they were being sold.

Our phone had been ringing incessantly since word got around that we had left CBN. Christian stations all over the country were asking for help with their telethons, and I began to feel as if God were leading me to help these stations in a free-lance capacity. That seemed like the only open door.

Dale Hill, who had become a close friend through our work at CBN, had visited several times since my resignation. We talked late into the night on several occasions about various concepts of reaching people for Christ by way of television. Dale had just returned from a hitch in the Army where the Lord had already sharpened his technical communications skills. He had come a long way from the sixteen-year old boy just off the farm he had been when he first joined CBN.

"I like your idea of working with Christian stations to help them get established," Dale said one night. "How do you plan to operate?"

"I'm not quite sure, but I think I should form a non-profit corporation to house my ministry. Other than that I'll wait on the Lord to open the doors to various stations."

Soon afterward, Marty Miller, who was general manager of a large metropolitan TV station, in Charlotte, showed up at our door with his wife Sarah. The Millers had both found Christ through the ministry of the "700 Club" and they were greatly impressed with the possibilities of Christian television. They encouraged me to form a non-profit corporation along the lines I had discussed with Dale Hill.

"Since you two already know about the legal work involved in forming a corporation," I suggested, "why don't you just join with us in one?"

"That sounds great," they both agreed. Sitting together around our kitchen table in Portsmouth with the Millers, Tammy and I formed Trinity Broadcasting Systems, to house my ministry and to aid Christian stations.

The new owners of our house were scheduled to move in December 8th and we had to be making plans. "Have you noticed how the number eight keeps coming up lately?" Tammy asked one day as we began to seek the Lord's guidance for the future.

"That's right," I said thinking about it. "We resigned on November 8th, the property will be closed out on December 8th, and we are working in our eighth year in broadcasting. I wonder what all this business with the number eight means?"

"I looked it up the other day in a concordance," she said

with a grin, "and the number eight signifies new beginnings in God."

"New beginnings, huh?" I mused. That sure sounded like us. We had resigned secure jobs at CBN to venture into the unknown with God. I felt a lot like Abraham who . . . "went out, not knowing whither he went" (Hebrews 11:8).

Tammy and I were both exhausted from the events of the last several months, and we desperately needed a rest. The Lord confirmed that "rest" one day while I was praying. *This prolonged rest will be your last until the coming of Jesus . . . for once you start again it will be intense work until the day of His appearing.*

Before leaving Portsmouth, we took the money from the sale of the house and purchased a new Avion travel trailer, and while the paper work was being processed on the new non-profit corporation, we vacationed on the Florida Keys over the Christmas holidays. It was a refreshing time, just as the Lord had prescribed.

Early in the new year, we drove to Greenville, South Carolina, to conduct a telethon with the Reverend James Thompson who had been a friend for many years. The Greenville telethon over WGGS, Channel 16, was a big success and quickly reached its goal in three days.

Dale Hill was working at Greenville to help upgrade the station's telecasts. "It looks as if you could have a real ministry traveling around to stations helping in their telethons," he remarked following the Greenville fund-raising effort.

"Yes, it does, Dale," I answered, "but we're still seeking God's will. I don't know what really lies ahead."

Next we went to Phoenix to do another weekend telethon. Once before the Lord had used us to keep this same station from going off the air, and once again it reached its goal as God continued to bless.

The Phoenix telethon's success was dimmed by news of my brother Bob's severely declining condition. Margie Klages, my cousin who had led Bob back to the Lord, called from Pasadena. "Bob's here with me," she said tearfully.

"Oh, my goodness," I said completely surprised. "How did he get out there?"

"He dragged himself onto an airplane and flew here from Tucson," she replied.

Somehow I could understand why. "You know, Margie," I said softly, "Bob always felt such love from you. I can see why he would want to be near you in his last moments."

"Jim, it really hasn't been a sad time in spite of Bob's condition," she said. "We've had prayer meetings continuously for over a week. I've invited my friends into the house, and we've sung and praised God. Bob has even sung, too."

At the end of the week, Bob was unable to travel back to Tucson by himself and Margie had to telephone my father in Michigan. He came out to bring Bob back to Tucson.

That night they were returning to Tucson, so Tammy and I drove to the airport. A thousand memories crowded into my thoughts as I watched plane after plane, jumbo jets and single engine props, take off into and land from the darkened sky.

When Bob's plane finally landed, everybody else on the flight deplaned and there was still no sign of Bob and my father. Then a large hydraulic lift moved alongside the plane and brought Bob down in a wheelchair. His eyes were shut. His hands hung down limply. He looked over a hundred years old. His body was a bag of skin and bones.

Watching the gray hydraulic lift come slowly down, James 1:15 came to mind . . . "and sin, when it is finished, bringeth forth death." Even though Bob would ultimately go home to be with the Lord—the sins of his life were bringing forth death in his physical body.

After we finally got my brother into the car, we drove slowly back towards the Veterans' Hospital. Bob was so weak he rested his head on my father's shoulder. Daddy lightly cradled him in his arms, "Bobby, I love you."

I had never heard my father call him Bobby before. It was probably a name the family had used when Bob was a small boy. As we drove along, love and remorse filled my mind with bittersweet thoughts of what might have been.

After Bob had strayed from the Lord, there had been a chance a few years earlier to turn him back when he visited Muskegon and daddy had convinced him to go to church. Once there, my father, being the head usher, asked Bob to help take up the offering that night. Unfortunately, the preacher's wife saw Bob with the offering plate, walked over to him and yanked it from his hands. To my knowledge, he never walked back inside the doors of a church after that incident.

But God's mercy extended into the depths of his bitterness and rebellion. Bob did see the love of God radiating through the eyes of his cousin Margie. That love was genuine, and he repented.

Bob died a few days after he returned from Los Angeles. He asked for no funeral services. His wish was that his body be cremated and his ashes strewn across the same mountains where I had walked a few months earlier with the Lord. His request was honored.

After leaving Arizona, Tammy and I visited with Margie in Pasadena and attended church services at Faith Center in nearby Los Angeles. Since our CBN shows had been telecast in the area, we were already known by the people and Ray Shock, the center's pastor, asked me to preach at the Sunday evening service. I had known Brother Shock for some time and had great appreciation for the work he had done in Faith Center, which included an excellent television ministry over Channel 30.

Paul Crouch, who had been assistant pastor of my home church in Muskegon, was working as general manager of Channel 30, and he and I had opportunity to share our ideas about Christian television. At the time I was even considering the possibility of joining Channel 30, if I had gotten a clear-cut invitation from Ray Shock.

"I'm looking to settle down again with my family," I told Paul. "We've been traveling three months doing telethons and it isn't satisfying any more."

Nodding his head, Paul concurred. "I've traveled a little myself. I know how draining it can be."

"I have to be frank, Paul," I said, "the way some of the stations are being operated bothers me. Wrestling, roller derbys and a host of other things are now being telecast over some of the Christian stations. It isn't right to raise money to support that kind of television."

"I'm with you on that," Paul said firmly, "that's not my idea of Christian television, either."

KBSA-TV, Channel 46, was available at the time and Paul began talking about leaving Faith Center and possibly joining hands with me in a new television venture. Paul's ideas about Christian television were compatible with mine. Could this be what the Lord had brought us to the West Coast to do? Start another late-night Christian talk show?

"I want to run the business end of the operation," Paul suggested, "and leave the ministering to somebody else."

"That sounds fine to me," I agreed. "I wouldn't be interested in the business end. I'd prefer to handle the ministry over the air."

"Well, what do you think?" he asked, pushing for an answer.

"I'm tremendously interested in the possibility," I answered, "but we have another telethon to do in Indianapolis. Why don't you join us in prayer about it, and we'll believe God for an answer when we get back in a week or two."

And that's the way we left it as Tammy and I drove off to

Indianapolis. The opportunity with Paul was the only door opening on the West Coast for us. We wanted to be sure Tammy and Jim Bakker would be in the will of God if they walked through that door.

At the telethon in Indianapolis with Lester Sumrall, God raised the budget and paid for two color cameras. Tammy and I rejoiced, and returned to Los Angeles. "We believe it's God's will to stay here and attempt to get a ministry off the ground," I told Paul by telephone.

"Great," he shouted. "I'll file the necessary papers."

We immediately applied for Channel 46. Using my non-profit corporation, Trinity Broadcasting Systems, we filed as an out-of-state corporation in California.

The station's owners were Bill Myers, an engineer and old-timer in broadcasting who possessed one of the first FCC licenses ever issued, and, believe it or not, a Philadelphia lawyer. Bill had built the station and owned fifty-one percent, the lawyer, forty-nine. Buying all or part of a station is not a simple matter because of the FCC paper work that usually takes one to three years to complete. In the meantime we would lease it from Bill and negotiate with the lawyer for his share.

The station was licensed for Guasti, a town in San Bernardino County right in the heart of the grape country. One day, after Paul had left Faith Center and we were waiting word on our application, Paul and I drove out to Guasti with our wives.

We finally found it on the map, and drove out the San Bernardino Freeway. We took a left on Archibald Avenue and then turned right on Valley Boulevard, the only street that runs through Guasti.

We found our way to the front door of a weather-beaten general store, one of Guasti's four buildings. The other three structures included a post office, a house with a white picket fence, and an old Spanish mission with statues dotting its courtyards. The buildings were arranged in a square surrounded by grape vineyards. Scattered through the vineyards were what looked to be migrant workers' houses.

The four of us walked into the general store for something cold to drink. "We're looking for the Guasti television studios," I told the sleepy-eyed clerk behind the counter.

He looked somewhat puzzled. "No hablo Ingles, senor," he replied.

"That's fine," I answered, "but do you know where Channel 46 is located?"

"No hablo," he repeated, adding a shrug of his shoulders.

And that was the same answer we got from everybody who came into the store. We finally realized that nobody in Guasti, California, could speak English. So the whole trip wouldn't be a waste, we walked across the street and prayed in the Spanish mission, asking for God's help in the project.

Thereafter, "What's a Guasti?" became a favorite expression. It sounded like some ice cream delight, but we were hoping it would become the name of a new television location for the Lord.

Late one night Paul called. "Jim," he said excitedly, "I've just gotten word, we have permission to begin broadcasting over KBSA."

"Praise the Lord!" I shouted into the phone, almost waking up Tammy.

"The only problem now," Paul added, "is getting the money to put the station on the air."

"God worked miracles at CBN with Pat Robertson's initial investment of three dollars," I responded. "He'll provide for us too."

Tammy and I had a thousand dollars left from the sale of our house, and Paul invested some of his money. Together with a few other contributions, we started getting Channel 46 ready to broadcast. I continually reminded myself, "It's not the amount of money I have—it's who God is. He's the source of all things."

And it was almost as if each time I reminded myself—a

still, small voice came back saying, "and with God all things are possible, only believe." I was daily believing God for a miracle to raise up the new television ministry.

13

Trouble
on the Tube

"This place is perfect for a television studio," I said surveying the one-time computer building located in an industrial park at Santa Ana. "It's a real gift from the Lord."

"That's right," Tammy answered as her voice echoed off the empty building's walls. "The glass-encased room back there that was originally set up for computers can now be used as our control room overlooking the studio."

I walked back past the new control room mentally planning the studio's layout. Another room off the main studio would house our equipment. Offices would be down the hall and a prop room across the hall with a sound barrier in the middle. Perfect.

"Boy, oh boy," I exclaimed. "We won't have to move a single wall. The building has been heavily wired for computers and is just right for air conditioning and our energy-draining equipment."

"There is one problem," Tammy was eyeing the floors.

"Yep, I can see that tile will have to come up," I said.

"Television cameras need a flat, hard surface. We could never get them across this."

Tammy and Paul's wife, Jan, charged into the job of removing the tile. Dressed in her Mickey Mouse tee shirt, Tammy made an interesting sight. The tile popped off easily enough, but underneath was a thick layer of tar. Puzzled at how to finish the job, the girls' work came to a stop. Minutes later, Duane Riddle, a local Assembly of God associate pastor, walked in with his wife.

"I've got just the chemical you need to dissolve that stuff," he said. "I'll be right back with it."

After one application, the hardened tar became a sea of black mud as the chemical began loosening it. Ultimately Tammy began wading out into the "sea" and scooping the black mess into big garbage cans lined with plastic bags. When the job was finished, everybody involved with the project looked like the "tar baby" from the Uncle Remus stories.

Each time we had a need, the Lord supplied it. One day before we started broadcasting, we needed to have a gas line moved in the building. "It would surely be nice to have a man from the gas company today," someone remarked. And before we knew it, a man from the gas company walked in.

While the building was being readied for use, we were also lining up a first-rate staff to occupy it. Putting in a call to Greenville, I told Dale Hill, "I could use your help in this new production studio in Los Angeles." Sensing the call of God in those few words, Dale was in California in a few days to direct our operations.

A month later, Sam Orender followed Dale to TBS where he became production manager. Director Roger Flessing had been working for a Christian station in Phoenix before he joined the staff, while art director Alex Valderrama had been employed in another station in California.

In television work, emphasis is normally placed on the picture over the sound, but at TBS we had decided to have studio quality sound as well. Someone on the staff had met Ralph Carmichael's son-in-law, Howard Steel, who designs custom-built audio boards for recording studios. Steel tipped us to an incredible purchase.

"Wolfman Jack," the popular acid rock disc jockey, had gone out of business on the West Coast and his custom-built, seven-foot-long audio board valued at $40,000 new was for sale at $8,000 cash.

"Some people have the idea that with a three-inch speaker in the television set, you don't need much sound," Roger Flessing said, "but since the Lord is providing, let's go for this piece of equipment."

Roger and Dale were convinced they could fit the audio board into our system, and, when the Lord provided the funds, we purchased the equipment. Here was an audio board once used for screaming rock music, soon to be used for the message of peace, love and joy—the message of Jesus.

As word began to spread around Los Angeles that Channel 46 was going on the air to broadcast the Christian story, contributions and help from all directions began pouring in. Office equipment, typewriters, desks, chairs, even the telephones were donated. An anonymous benefactor made arrangements through the PTL Telephone Company—of all names—to handle our phones free of charge.

Near the end of May 1973, we were almost ready to begin broadcasting when we realized there was a missing ingredient in our plans: no television cameras!

"Do you have any idea where we might borrow some cameras?" I asked Paul who had lived in the Los Angeles area for some time.

Paul shook his head. "I can't really think of anybody, Jim," he answered, "especially since we'll be needing them almost seven days a week."

The situation looked pretty glum. "Wait a minute," Paul

said after a few minutes. "I could check with Ralph Wilkerson at Melodyland. They did have a regular program awhile back, but I'm not sure what they are doing presently."

Paul contacted Ralph. "Could we use your cameras on a temporary basis while we're starting up the program?" Paul asked.

"Sure, they're just sitting in the church right now," came the reply. And in short order, Channel 46 was ready to go on the airwaves.

Just prior to hitting the air in Los Angeles, I received a call from Marty Miller in Charlotte. "Ted Turner, the station's owner, wants to carry your program over Channel 36 here," he said. "Can you start shipping us tapes of your show?"

"We can ship the tapes," I answered, "but there will be a delay since we haven't started producing the program yet, and really don't have any video equipment either."

A few days later the Millers, who were still part of our non-profit corporation, flew to California and we had a board of directors meeting at Paul Crouch's house. Paul and his wife, Jan, were added to the board. The Millers would head up the East Coast business for Trinity Broadcasting Systems and the Crouches, the West Coast. I would continue as president.

Using the late-night talk show concept, the program was finally inaugurated in Los Angeles. We called it the "PTL Club."

Tammy and I together with the Crouches had come up with the name. We had wanted something that would be a code name to the Christian world, but which would not turn off lost people. "What's wrong with the 'Praise the Lord' show?" Tammy had asked.

"With a religious sounding name like that, I wouldn't have a chance to present the gospel to some people," I answered, "and, after all, that's our goal, to reach the lost for Jesus."

"So why don't we shorten it to PTL?" Paul questioned.

"That's good," I said with a snap of my fingers. "PTL is

a sign to most Christians. And it's not a dead giveaway that the program's religious."

When the "PTL Club" came on, people throughout the greater Los Angeles area began responding and we soon were receiving reports of healing, miracles and salvation.

We broadcast about five hours or more each evening beginning around seven o'clock, depending on a microwave problem that continually hampered our signal. The inversion layer and the Los Angeles smog combined to give our technicians fits. Sometimes, in the middle of the program, the picture would fade out for a few seconds and then slowly fade back in. Part of the problem came from the fact that we had to get the signal from Santa Ana up to the broadcast tower on Mount Wilson.

One night the control room received a call from Bill Myers, the channel's owner who operated from the broadcast tower on Mount Wilson. "We're having audio problems with the program," he told Roger Flessing, "we'll have to go off the air temporarily." People on camera were all talking normally, but the sound wasn't coming through the sets at home.

In turn, Roger told Alex to "make up a sign." In a few seconds a sign reading: "We're having trouble with the audio portion of the program. We'll be back in five minutes" was flashed on the screen.

Bill came back on the line. "No way," he said, "we'll be off at least a half-hour."

Roger cupped his hand over the phone's mouthpiece and shouted back to Alex. "Hey, Alex," he yelled, "make that thirty minutes."

With the camera still focused on the sign, a hand belonging to Alex came in from the right side of the screen, scratched out five, wrote in thirty and waved to the audience.

Back on the phone, Bill said to Roger, "That's the funniest thing I've ever seen," and hung up.

Working with inexperienced cameramen was almost as much fun as wrestling with the ongoing technical difficulties. We had asked continually over the air for volunteers to operate the cameras, and that's what we got: volunteers. People frequently walked into the studios asking what they could do, and we immediately placed them behind a camera with instructions to just "aim."

I had to alert the crew ahead of time if I planned to move around on the set by saying, "I'm going to stand up now." If I didn't, the cameraman might end up with a beautiful shot of my belt buckle.

We had only been on the air a short time and sending tapes to Charlotte, when Paul and I flew there to participate in their annual telethon. A few nights later Tammy called from California in tears.

"Melodyland needed their camera equipment back," she said. "We're without cameras!"

The station managed to stay on the air only through the technicians' ingenuity and the grace of God. Melodyland had left a small Sony graphics camera, the type used in closed circuit operations. And for several weeks, until we got back to California and worked out an arrangement for new cameras, the staff used that one camera five nights a week. It was a miracle!

In spite of these and many other apparently insuperable problems, people by the score were getting saved, healed and baptized with the Holy Spirit. And the viewers' generosity was heaven-sent. Everytime we had a need at the station, the people responded. Once our microphones were falling apart. We told the viewers, and they quickly sent enough money to provide truly superior equipment.

But the crucial time came when the staff faced a salary crunch. People on the staff had made unbelievable sacrifices to help get Channel 46 on the air—some had come across country to California. Most everybody was working from nine o'clock in the morning until whenever the "PTL Club" went off at night. And salaries were low, very low. In fact, as president, I was drawing only a hundred dollars a week.

One night, the staff had just about reached the straining point with salaries, and I felt God wanted me to tell the audience about it.

"I want the video tape men, directors, producers, everybody who is behind the scenes to come up front," I said. "Lock down the cameras."

Everybody on the staff stepped in front of the cameras, and I introduced them one by one explaining exactly what each person's job entailed and what they were personally sacrificing to be there.

"We need to pay these people," I said emotionally. "We need to pay some bills as well. We need a lot of money. If you want to mail it, that's fine. But if you want to bring it down tonight, you can even do that. That way you can say thanks to these people for their contributions to this community."

And with that someone placed a large fishbowl in the middle of the studio floor, and the Spirit of God began speaking to people. In short order, people were crowding in and out of the studio bringing contributions. Most of the people came with tears in their eyes.

At one point, a volunteer cameraman endorsed his check from a regular job and tossed it into the fishbowl. "God," I prayed as I watched the people bringing in their gifts, "bless these people for their obedience."

Broadcasting five hours a night, seven days a week, we had plenty of time for guests and singing groups. Volunteers came regularly to help by answering phones and praying with the callers.

But each time we were about to gain a significant victory, some of the local pastors would show up at the studio wanting to talk—right while we were on the air.

Paul constantly tried to get me off the set to talk with these men. I felt like Nehemiah when he asked, "Why should the work cease, whilst I leave it, and come down to you?" (Nehemiah 6:3). I was exasperated.

One night during our telethon in the early fall, I was on the air making an appeal and the contributions were pouring in. One of the local pastors arrived and Paul put him on the air. I could hardly believe my ears.

"I know this thing hasn't been run right," he said, "but we're going to change that!"

I walked dejectedly out of the studio and sat down alone in a prop room. I was losing the television ministry in Los Angeles. I had thought it was going to be *my* ministry for the rest of my life, and I had put everything I had into it.

That's where I was wrong. I thought it was "my ministry" rather than God's, and I couldn't release it.

My heart broke and I bawled. I was still in the prop room crying when Tammy found me sometime later. I was sobbing uncontrollably.

Tammy knew almost immediately what was happening. "Jim," she said softly, "Jesus died in obedience to the Father. They killed Him. But those words people have said against you won't kill you."

"That's not it," I said shaking my head. "I've touched the ark, holding on too tightly."

I felt like there was nothing in the world to live for anymore. Would Tammy and Tammy Sue be taken too? God knew how I'd hung onto them. My whole world had suddenly crumbled on top of me.

Tammy left briefly and returned with Tammy Sue. The three of us huddled in that prop room crying and hugging for some time.

"If God takes this away," Tammy finally said to me, "He has something else. You know that He never wounds but that He won't bind up. We're still His servants. Even if God wants us out of Christian television, we can do it.''

After that experience, the gap widened almost daily between Paul and myself. The unity and mutual agreement of programming concepts rapidly began to collapse.

I continued to be the subject of seemingly endless criticism. ''I don't think you should pray for the sick over television,'' one pastor would remark. ''I don't think you should minister in the Spirit over television,'' another suggested. While a third would say, ''I don't think you ought to have this kind of music on the show. Why don't you try another kind?''

You will never please everybody when you're in a public marketplace like television. The Lord had convinced me of that at CBN. I was just one man. I couldn't please everybody. That was impossible. But the criticism hurt just the same. How I wished they would leave me alone. I was there trying to reach an audience for Jesus, and I expected other people to reach their audience for Him, too. But God's hand was on me to chasten and cleanse.

In the early fall, our operation switched from Channel 46 to Channel 40. The former channel was taken over by a Baptist group headed by Reverend Ken Connelly. The change brought a great improvement in our signal and ultimately increased our viewing audience.

From the very start of our ministry in Los Angeles, I had told our viewing audience that the station would not be owned and operated by a single church. It would be for all the people who wanted to support it. And it would be interdenominational. I felt it was the way I could be most effective for Christ. The Lord had told me, while alone on that mountain in Arizona, to work within the denominations. I wanted to work with all the churches and favor none.

But in a board of directors meeting one day in November, a proposal was set forward to put the ministry under the umbrella of a single church in order to get our license from the FCC. I argued strongly against the proposal.

"It's not that I am opposed to any church," I explained, "but what you are asking me to do would make me a liar. I can't do that."

The board's vote was five to one. I was the lone dissenting vote.

Immediately, the board asked for my resignation. "That's fine," I said almost expecting the situation to come to this. I went into my office and with my secretary's help began putting some things into boxes.

One of our lawyers stopped by my office on his way out of the building. "Jim," he said sincerely, "if you feel what you're doing is right, you ought to stick with your decision. Otherwise you ought to try to stay."

"Thanks," I answered, "but it looks like God wants me out."

I left the studio that day not knowing what Jim Bakker would do, or whether he'd ever be back on television again. Whatever small savings I had was now gone. Everything I had worked the last several months for was gone. I was broke, unemployed and a failure.

Once again, I found myself having to give up. It was God's way.

14

The Tie that Binds

November 1973. A big percentage of the staff resigned their jobs with me that day. They knew about my conflict with the board of directors and agreed with me that no one church should own the television ministry.

Meeting at my home a few days later, all of us who had quit sat around looking at one another. "Okay Lord, what do we do now?" was the unspoken question on everyone's lips. Since most of the men's wives had also worked at the station, there wasn't a gainfully employed person among us. We were all broke and out-of-work.

That day while we were praying, Tammy began to cry. She appeared to be getting some word from the Lord.

Through a choking voice, she described a vivid scene, "For as far as I could see, angels were flying back and forth. They wore large metal helmets and the Lord Jesus stood before me facing the angels. I noticed his robe had bright colors of blue and white. It was the most shining cloth I'd ever seen."

"Then, Jesus turned to me, *Tammy, even as you are standing here, my angels are going forward to do battle for you—so you don't need to worry about anything—only believe in Me.*"

Everybody in the room broke out in spontaneous praise to God. "That confirms the words that God has been speaking to my own heart," I shared. "The Lord reminded me of Philippians 4:6,7 which says, 'Be careful for nothing; but in everything by prayer and supplication with thanksgiving let your requests be made known unto God. And the peace of God, which passeth all understanding, shall keep your hearts and minds through Christ Jesus.'

"Worry is a negative force and we're all guilty of doing it from time to time. But we've got to keep our guard up against worry because it presents a barrier to hearing the Lord . . . and in the shape we're in we've got to hear God to survive.

"This is a spiritual battle we are in and we must use the weapons of the Spirit: prayer, fasting, and supplication," I added.

As the first of December approached, I realized our sizable house payment was coming due, and we didn't have the money to pay it. One morning I was sitting in the bathtub soaking and praying over the matter when I heard Tammy burst through the front door and begin running up the stairs. "Jim, Jim," she shouted.

I jumped out of the tub thinking the house must be on fire. Before I could think twice, Tammy was in the room gasping for breath. "Jim," she said excitedly, "look what the Lord has given us!"

She was holding a bank statement in her hand. "It's a statement saying we've got $1,500 in our checking account that we didn't know we had," she exclaimed.

"What?"

"It's from our bank back in Portsmouth," she explained. "Somehow we made an error in our checking account when we left Virginia and the error amounted to $1,500 in our favor."

The Tie that Binds

We were unaccustomed to dealing with large sums of money, and when we had sold our house and furnishings, we had—it now appeared—made an enormous error in subtraction.

And for the next two months, miracle after miracle was the order of the day. Not just for us—but for the twenty poeple who had left Channel 40 with us.

When friends across the state learned we were no longer with the station, they began sending contributions to us daily. We were amazed—and overcome—by the love God showered on us in our weak and dependent state. Cards and letters continually arrived with contributions at a rate of over a thousand dollars a week, enabling us to pay each member of the staff his normal paycheck.

Herter Backland, a Christian woman who owned three Swedish-style restaurants, each known as Villa Sweden, gave our staff a standing invitation to her delicious smorgasbord. "Free meals for as long as you want any time you want," she said happily.

Ella Eix and her son Freddie began stocking my freezer with some of the finest cuts of meat money could buy. "I have to pray every time you folks drive up," I laughed one day when Ella and Freddie were again stuffing my refrigerator, "to find space for all the food you're bringing over here."

"It's not us doing it; it's the Lord." We constantly gave the food away to staff members and yet it was never depleted because the Eixes always brought more.

As Christmas time neared, Ann Stribanek donated $500 in gift certificates to everybody—so Tammy and I made the rounds of the May Company department store buying presents. Another friend, Carole Taylor, bought several gifts for each member of the staff.

With some fifty people in attendance, we had our Christmas party at Villa Sweden. Later, everybody drove to our house to open the presents that were piled high underneath the tallest Christmas tree we could buy. "This is one of the most exciting

Christmases of my life,'' Tammy exuded while everybody was opening their gifts.

"I agree," I smiled. "This has got to be the holiday to end all holidays. It's like God's special gift to each of us. We'll remember this as the Christmas that Jesus gave us."

Months before, I had met composer Paul Mickelson when he appeared on the "PTL Club." I had known of him since my CBN days when I had played his records over radio, so I was a little nervous when I stepped out into the hall, at the studio, that night to meet Paul before the program. There were three women dressed in fur coats standing with him. "My goodness, he has an entourage with him," I thought to myself.

But once we got acquainted, I could see Paul wasn't the kind of person to have an entourage, and certainly these people were anything but society matrons. In fact, the women were Mrs. Mickelson, Fern Luther and Judy Chavez, who, Paul later told me on the show, was an evangelist and that I should interview her.

And with that, Judy had come on the program. She had a God-given ability to motivate people in faith. Judy's appeal was so universally accepted that we created a program in motivating faith that was highly successful. Unfortunately when we went off the air, so did Judy's program.

After we left Channel 40 we met nightly in our home for prayer. Judy gave us strong messages about faith during those meetings. Every person on the staff had no choice but to walk in faith, and Judy's Bible-centered teachings were encouragement indeed.

Money continued coming in. People constantly brought it to the prayer meetings. Surprisingly enough, staff members who had always been behind the scenes at the television station had total strangers walk up and give them money. God was providing every need, from rent or mortgage payments down to Christmas presents and food. He didn't leave anything out.

As my birthday (January 2nd) approached, Paul Mickelson

called to invite several of us to Palm Springs for the New Year's holiday. Paul had friends there who were sole heirs to the Upjohn pharmaceutical fortune, and we stayed in their home.

The night after we arrived everybody gathered in one of the house's large rooms, and Paul sat down at a theatre-style pipe organ. Another man played an electric organ while a third played the piano, and they all joined in playing "Happy Birthday" to me.

Tammy and I sat on a couch nearby as tears of joy stained both of our faces. "God," I said out loud, "You really know how to treat Your people."

"Amen," Tammy responded. "Here we are broke and unemployed, yet God has housed us with a millionaire and treated us to the best restaurants in Palm Springs." It was a birthday I would never forget.

During those three months of November, December and January, our staff, Dale Hill, Sam Orender, Roger Flessing, Alex Valderrama and Del Holford, met daily to pray and plan. The technicians even began making plans for a television remote truck. We didn't know if we would ever have use for such a truck, but the guys believed we would—so we began asking God for one.

They likewise began drawing up wiring diagrams for a first-class television studio, believing the Lord one day would provide this, too.

Help continued to be offered from all kinds of sources. Ruth and Rio Stinson opened their home to us to use as an office while Paul and Loretta Mays frequently helped out in our makeshift office. Bethel Perry handled all the bookkeeping chores. Norman Carl, Jean Duncan, Beverly Norberg, Beverly McIntyre, Maury Dahlen and Clyde Gilbert and a host of others stood together with us.

God was doing more, though, than providing everyone's needs, he was also assembling a working team. "I'd like to be part of a body of people working together without any big shots around," someone suggested one day.

"I think that's probably the unspoken prayer of each one here," I answered while we all looked around, nodding in agreement.

Tammy and I might have been the people on camera, but we never considered ourselves more important than the other staff members. From my earliest days in broadcasting, I recognized that without a production crew we wouldn't have had a ministry on television.

Our common bond in Christ was incalculably strengthened as, during that three-month interval, we walked together in faith and suffered the pain of utter uncertainty. We had all gladly seen the hand of God raising up the television ministry in Los Angeles . . . but even more, we had seen and experienced His life when we left that ministry. Surely the struggles we shared united us as nothing else could.

God had picked up the broken pieces of the Los Angeles television ministry and made a new and stronger team. But for what? I wondered.

15

Charlotte

When I was hosting the "PTL Club" in Los Angeles, video tapes of the program were being telecast three days a week over WRET, Channel 36, in Charlotte. The other two days a week a local program called the "Praise the Lord" show was being produced through the efforts of Marty and Sarah Miller.

Marty was general manager of WRET which, however, was a regular commercial station owned by Turner Communications Corporation. Marty and Sarah did the "Praise the Lord" program on the side, you might say.

Charlotte's annual telethon was scheduled in late January 1974 and the Millers telephoned asking me to handle the fund-raising effort. Tammy and I drove cross-country to North Carolina for what we thought would be a two-week stay.

The Downings, some of gospel music's most popular singers, were part of the opening night festivities at Ovens Auditorium. Years before the group was just starting out when they appeared with me in Portsmouth about the time "700 Club" was being launched. I recalled those early days as Tammy and I waited backstage that night.

"Ladies and gentlemen . . ." Tammy and I were about to be introduced and I noticed she was extremely nervous. I reached to clasp her hand and reassure her.

". . . would you give a great big Charlotte welcome to Jim and Tammy Bakker!"

The curtains parted slightly and we walked out into a packed house of some 2600 people, and, before I knew it, the entire audience was on its feet cheering and clapping. Tammy and I were taken completely by surprise. We were overwhelmed.

Tears flowed freely down both of our faces as I tried to thank the people. "We're so grateful to be with you tonight," I said tearfully, "and sense the presence of God in this place."

The audience roared its approval.

The Lord's presence was incredibly real that night and as Tammy began singing "The Blood Will Never Lose Its Power," people began rejoicing and shouting throughout the auditorium. More than two hundred walked to the front that night to receive Jesus as their Savior.

Because of scheduling problems, the telethon from WRET's studios didn't begin until late Friday night, but the minute we hit the air and began praying for the sick, God began to work powerfully.

I didn't recognize the extent of the Holy Spirit's move until I noticed the slips of paper piling up on my desk with reports of various healings. As I began reading these slips over the air they seemed to release people's faith and the miracles multiplied.

"We've received a call from a lady in Charlotte who was being treated for a large goiter," I read from a report, "and after prayer tonight that goiter has disappeared!"

The reports seemed to be coming in almost as fast as I could read them . . . arthritis healed, kidney problem healed, bad back healed, problem with eyesight healed, loss of hearing healed, sinus healed. Tumors and cancers were dropping off people's bodies. Hundreds were calling the station for prayer . . . for healing . . . for salvation . . . and to pledge support to the fledgling television ministry.

Miracle after miracle was being reported. As amazing as were the continual healings God was performing, the numbers of people accepting Christ was equally stunning. From late Friday night until Sunday night, more than five hundred people received Jesus. It seemed as if God had unleashed the bomb of his Holy Spirit on the metropolitan Charlotte, North Carolina area—a city rooted in the South's Bible belt—yet deeply in need of a spiritual renewal.

John Gimenez, who together with his wife, Ann, pastors the Rock Church in the Tidewater area, were part of the telethon team. One night as the Lord led John to pray for a woman to receive the Baptism with the Holy Spirit on the air, people throughout the area began to receive it as well.

Phoned response to the telethon was so great that twenty-five counselors and staff members were not sufficient to handle all the calls. Tammy and I answered phones whenever possible as the station was simply deluged.

I picked up one phone and a lady said to me, "Jim, I've been praying for you and Tammy since I saw you at the Full Gospel Businessmen's meeting in September 1972 here. I felt God was trying to bring you to Charlotte. There are people who will support you and pray for you in this city."

Throughout the weekend, I received a number of such calls. After answering another like it, I looked over at Tammy who was just finishing up with a conversation over the phone.

"Have you gotten any unusual phone calls?" I asked, walking over to where she was sitting.

"Yeah," she answered with a grin, "people are praying that we'd come to Charlotte."

For several days after the telethon, I isolated myself and

began seeking the Lord for some answers. If God planned a change in our lives, I needed to know. Tammy and I, plus the production crew and their families, had waited more than three months in Los Angeles for doors to open and yet no really open door was in view. Could Charlotte be where God wanted us?

How much clearer do I have to make it? the still, inner voice said. *I want you here. This is the vineyard I've placed before you and your obedience will bear much fruit.*

Once again, I felt the Lord leading us and we decided to move from California to Charlotte. The "Praise the Lord" program was only being telecast over one station in one city, but I believed that God knew what He was doing. I needed only to obey His voice.

I flew back to California and put our house up for sale. Since Tammy had decorated the house with pictures from top to bottom, I knew there would be countless holes in the walls. So, I delayed moving the furniture out while prospective buyers were looking the house over.

The house was sold within three days and some of our production crew moved the furniture out while I flew back to North Carolina. I had just arrived and dived headlong into the new work when Tammy called the office.

"The real estate people called from California," she said. "The sale of our house fell through."

"Oh, Lord," I said dejectedly. I could picture that house bare of the furniture and the walls full of holes. It would be much harder to sell than before. I began to worry about having to make two house payments since I had already bought a home in Charlotte. Anxiety sprang up within me very quickly, considering how much I had been exercised in faith during the previous few months.

"Oh, I'll never make it now," I sighed, thinking about this newest problem.

For months I had been preaching Psalm 37:3-5 to everyone within earshot, including Tammy: "Trust in the Lord . . . Delight thyself also in the Lord . . . Commit thy way unto the Lord.''

"Wait a minute," Tammy said sharply, "you've been preaching that once we've committed a problem to God, we ought not to take it again. You've got to practice what you preach.''

Humbled by Tammy's words, I realized my mistake as she preached my sermon back to me. As we prayed together I said, "Lord, I commit this to You. If I go to the poor house, You're going with me. This is Your problem and I give it to You.''

Within twenty-four hours I received another call from California. The house had been resold for a thousand dollars more than I had paid for it.

Tim Kelton, a Charlotte pastor, and Jim Moss, a layman who donated most of his time to the television ministry, were serving as hosts of the "Praise the Lord" program. In February, I replaced them and Tammy began putting in a regular appearance on the program to sing and share.

One day I was getting my office arranged at the new studio on Independence Boulevard. Tammy was helping me. Jim Moss tapped lightly on the door, "Can I come in?"

"Sure," I answered.

"I just want you to understand one thing," he said taking a seat, "I'm with you one hundred per cent. If I've got something to say to you, I'll bring it out in the open and I want you to be the same with me.''

I appreciated his candor. "Since you've put it that way," I responded, "I've wondered how you feel about us coming from California and taking you out of the host spot on the show.''

Moss smiled, "I don't care about hosting. I never felt the Lord called me to host the program. As I see it, my position would be to help you. I'd like to get the guests on the show and work behind the scenes.''

"Great," I said, "I want you to produce the show."

"Is that what a producer is?" he asked. "I've seen that title on television screens, but I thought it was somebody with a bunch of money on his hip who produced the show through money."

"In some cases that's true, but in Christian television you're much more," I said. "You arrange for the guests and bring it all together in the studio. You work closely with me."

"Man, that's what I want to do," he said excitedly.

Moss was giving up a lucrative cleaning supply business to join the ministry. David Carver, a college graduate from Florida who had majored in broadcasting, joined us as a producer-director. Together with Dale Hill and Sam Orender of our California team, they would be the nucleus of our staff.

For the third time in less than ten years, Tammy and I were starting all over again.

16

"A Call Poured In!"

When I came to Charlotte, work began on a newly-leased building at 6500 East Independence Boulevard to transform it into television studios. Originally built as a furniture showroom and later converted into office space, the building was perfectly suited for our needs with offices in the front portion and several workshop-sized rooms in the rear.

"The only problem I see," said Dale Hill as we walked through one of the large back rooms, "is that we'll have to gut the ceilings to get enough height for the lights."

Dale was right. "But there's one good thing this building has over the one in California," I said pointing to the floor.

"That's right," Dale answered, "no tile to remove from this concrete floor."

I wanted to get set up in the new building as soon as possible. Dale, who had become a close brother in Christ over the years of mutual struggling, almost read my thoughts. "But, it's going to take a while to get in here, Jim," he said. "There's a lot of work involved in this and we may end up having to move some walls as well.''

I realized the obstacles we faced, but after I had seen, first-hand, the miracle God had performed at CBN and then watched another similar feat in California—I was ready to believe the Lord all over again.

I began explaining our needs to the viewers. One day I described the need for "a good professional organ and piano." Before the program left the air two hours later, over $5,000 had been pledged.

Then I told about the need for carpenters, painters and able-bodied men to help in the construction of the new facilities. That simple appeal brought the workmen we needed almost immediately.

Louis Sustar and his son, Jimmy, who made their living as carpenters, were among the first to volunteer their services. Wade Robinson, a Wesleyan Methodist preacher who didn't believe in the Baptism with the Holy Spirit, also volunteered.

"I might not agree with your doctrine," Wade told Jim Moss, "but I see the results of what you're doing and I like them." Wade brought along his son-in-law, Jeff Rikard, a hard-working carpenter who ultimately joined our staff to handle a variety of jobs. David Austin, another area pastor, came down to help. "I'll put down my Bible temporarily," he said, "just to pick up a hammer and nails to help God's work."

Because the volunteers had regular jobs and we were all tied up during the day with the program, we could work only at night on the new studios. Every night we worked on the building and had prayer meetings. People were being healed and baptized with the Spirit as the studios were put into shape.

"The first room that should be finished is the chapel," I said one night, "even before the staff offices are completed." Everybody nodded in agreement. "That's the most important room in the place," someone suggested.

"A Call Poured In!"

One night while the chapel was being put together, Jim Moss was talking with David Austin, Wade Robinson and Chip Southern, a young boy who had just received Christ a few days earlier. Chip suddenly spoke up, "I think we should lay hands on Brother Wade and pray for him."

And as they did, Wade fell gently to the floor under the power of God. Minutes later he awoke speaking in tongues. "I feel like a new man," he shouted, "I've never felt like this before in my life. I know what you're talking about now. The baptism is for real."

Wade began running around the room praising God and singing. It was one of the most dramatic baptisms any of us had ever seen.

Three months later, in late April, the response to the ministry was increasing almost daily and we scheduled a rally at Ovens Auditorium with the Happy Goodman Family. Vestal Goodman, one of the most beloved women in gospel music, was being treated for a heart condition at the time and was unable to leave the group's bus to appear on stage.

Finally, two women went outside to pray with her and Vestal consented to come on stage. When she walked out, I could see by her glassy eyes and pale complexion that she was sick. She tried to sing "God Walks These Dark Hills," but it lacked life.

Nearly 2600 people united in prayer for her that night with Jim Moss and members of our staff. "Unless God undertakes," I said, "Vestal Goodman might go home to be with the Lord."

Vestal originally had heart surgery in Nashville but days after we had prayed for her she checked into the Mayo Clinic for tests. Doctors there made an incredible discovery. "The doctors couldn't even find a trace of heart trouble," Vestal told me later, "in fact they couldn't even find a scar where I had been operated on." God had healed her condition and she was restored totally.

A few days later, we had scheduled another rally at the

143

Virginia Beach Dome, the place where God had performed some of the greatest miracles of my ministry and where Tammy was ultimately healed of her fear and depression. Leasing three buses, we filled them with some of our prayer partners and drove up from Charlotte.

Reservations had been made at the New Castle Motel on the beach, and that night, before the meeting, everybody met in the owner's apartment to pray. Mrs. Iscar Cobb welcomed the group and told us how God had given the business to her. Then she asked, "I wonder how many of us are gathered here to pray?"

The number came to 120—the same number that were together in the upper room on the day of Pentecost when the Holy Spirit was first poured out.

At the Dome, John Gimenez was in charge of the service and after a few brief announcements he introduced Rick Webb, a singer who was a friend of Jim Moss. Rick began singing an inspiring song, "Rise and Be Healed." After singing the song twice, the Rock Church choir joined in and the Spirit of God began quietly filling the auditorium. The song was repeated countless times as people reverently raised their hands in praise to God.

The power of God was present to heal, and after Rick and the choir finished singing, I began calling out various sicknesses that God was healing all over the auditorium. "The power of God is here tonight, people," I proclaimed. "He's here to do the impossible for you! Believe Him tonight and it will happen!"

By this time, practically every person in the auditorium who could stand was on his feet praising the Lord.

Jim Moss's wife, George Anna, was in the audience that night. A recent pap test had disclosed that she had cancer. Not only had the cancer begun to rapidly drain the strength from her body, but she had become pitifully depressed.

I walked across the platform toward her. She stood in the first row with Jim and I extended my hand toward her to pray, and as I did, it appeared a bolt of lightning shot from the tips of my fingers and hit her. Her body literally was picked up and hurtled through the air.

Moss rushed to her side and began praying over her. Ten minutes later when she came to, it was obvious that God had performed a miracle. The healing was confirmed later by her doctor in Charlotte. The second pap test was negative.

The healing service was completed as the three bus drivers walked to the front to give their hearts to the Lord. One of the drivers, a young man, had been cocky and self-assured all the while he had driven us to Virginia Beach, but the meeting at the Dome had shaken him completely. As I reached out to pray for him, he was slain in the Spirit and the auditorium went into an uproar.

Getting back to Charlotte, work was rapidly continuing on the studios with less than a month to finish everything before our first telethon in the new building. One night, Dale and I drew the plans for the studio set with the desks for the host and phone counselors. "Can you build it?" I asked, turning to Louis Sustar. "No problem," he said confidently. With the aid of his son Jimmy, Keith Rogers and other volunteers, Louis began putting the set together.

Only hours before the telethon was scheduled to begin, workers were slapping paint on the walls and running cables through the studio. Many of the staff members had worked through the last night to get the studio ready to broadcast.

Larry Sitton, our audio man, was operating one of the cameras for the first telethon. That night, ten minutes before we were scheduled to go on the air, his camera slipped off its tripod.

"Oh!" everybody screamed.

Larry tried to catch the camera, but managed only to hit the floor under the camera about the same time the 100-pound instrument fell. Larry was so shaken by the near catastrophe with the precious piece of equipment, he broke down and cried.

Roger Wilson, who had joined us three months earlier as

chief engineer, walked over hurriedly and lifted the camera back on its tripod. "There's only a broken wire," Roger announced after examining the camera.

Jim Moss went over to pray for Larry who was still weeping. "I need you, Larry," Moss said. "I need your help in this telethon so you've got to pull yourself together." Larry did.

The Downings, who had been with us at the January telethon, appeared again and greatly blessed everyone. Sunday night as the pledges slowed down to a trickle I made an announcement. "We'd like to have 200 people who will pledge ten dollars a month," I said. "If we don't get all 200 within the next hour, we won't accept any of them. Each one of the 200 is vitally important to this ministry. We can't do without any of you!"

Within an hour, we had the 200 pledges, but we had just made it by the skin of our teeth. While the Downings were singing another number, I rested momentarily and began sharing a story with some of the staff. "Have you ever heard the story of the man who crossed Niagara Falls on a bicycle?" I asked.

Everybody shook their heads.

"Well, after he did it once this man asked the people who had watched him do it if they believed he could cross the falls on a tightrope. Everybody agreed he could to it. 'Do *you* really believe I can do it,' he asked one of the men. 'Yeah, you can do it,' the man answered. 'In that case, get on my shoulders and I'll ride you across,' the stunt man said. 'Oh, no,' the other man replied."

Everybody chuckled.

The Downings completed their song and as I walked back on camera, the Lord began speaking to me. *Believe me for 300 partners at ten dollars a month,* he said.

"Lord, we just made it by the skin of our teeth last time," I lamented.

Do you trust me? the Lord asked.

"Yes," I answered.

"A Call Poured In!"

Get on my shoulders then, the Lord said, *and I'll ride you across.*

Back on camera, I got on God's shoulders. "We're going to believe God for 300 partners at ten dollars a month," I announced. "Just like before, we won't take any of them if we don't get all of them."

Words of uncertainty began popping up in my mind. "You're a fool. You're going to have to rip up all those pledges in front of those people. You're a fool."

But within thirty minutes, we had 300 pledges, then it rose to 400 and finally to 500. *You have obeyed me in faith,* the Lord spoke to me. *I don't want you to ask for any more money. You let me do it.*

And for the next two hours, I sat down on the couch and watched as pledges and contributions poured in. "You folks do what God tells you," I suggested . . . and thousands of dollars flooded into the station.

The Downings sang and played in the background as I read the pledges. The couch was filled with them. No prodding. No challenges. Nothing. And $100,000 had been pledged.

Right on the heels of that telethon, negotiations were completed for our first affiliate in Chattanooga and we scheduled a telethon after the broadcast had been airing for several weeks. The Downings, John and Ann Gimenez, the Jim Pierce Trio and our entire staff traveled to Chattanooga for the telethon. A special set had even been constructed for the appeal. We were all eager to get started.

I preached. John preached. The Downings sang. Tammy sang. People testified. Everybody poured their hearts out. And nothing happened. The program was also being broadcast on radio and that didn't help either.

Saturday afternoon, I drove off in my car to pray in the

hopes God would reveal something to me. That didn't even help much. When I returned to the station, Dale Hill greeted me. "Hey, Jim," he said, "a call just poured in!"

We all began to laugh, and that's about the way the whole telethon went. It was a colossal failure. The station's signal was so weak and inferior that our potential viewing audience was practically nothing. Everyone who could get the station's signal was at the station!

"Well," I said to Tammy as we drove back to Charlotte, "I've learned one thing from this trip. We will certainly research our stations in the future before signing any more contracts."

Two months later, in September, we signed WKAB, Channel 32 in Montgomery, Alabama. In October, we added WDXR, Channel 29, in Paducah, Kentucky to our list of affiliates. Prayer requests, phone calls and contributions soon began coming in from Alabama and Kentucky.

In November, we scheduled a rally in Mooresville, a town about thirty miles north of Charlotte. Wade Robinson was with me that night on the platform as we prayed for people. We prayed for hours that night. When I finally returned home, it was almost two o'clock in the morning and I was weary.

The phone broke the stillness of the early morning hours. Sleepily Tammy answered. It was Wade Robinson's daughter, Sandy. "They've just rushed my father to the emergency room," she cried, "please pray."

Tammy and I immediately asked God to heal whatever condition Wade had. The conversation with Sandy had been so hurried Tammy didn't have time to ask what had happened.

Minutes later Sandy called again. She was sobbing heavily. "Daddy's gone to be with the Lord," she said. "He had a heart attack and was dead on arrival at the hospital."

After calling several members of the staff with the news, I tried to go back to sleep, but couldn't. Finally I slipped out of bed and walked into the living room. Tammy had been reading her Bible that afternoon, and it was still open on the coffee table.

I picked it up and looked at what she had been reading. She had underlined the words of Jesus from John 11:25, 26. "I am the resurrection, and the life: he that believeth in me, though he were dead, yet shall he live: And whosoever liveth and believeth in me shall never die."

Wade Robinson had been in the ministry for many years when he joined our television outreach and his life had dramatically changed. Everyone who had known him, loved him. But I knew Wade wasn't dead. As a believer in Jesus, he would never die.

"Do you have any idea how much?" I asked.

He shook his head. "It could be ten dollars or ten million dollars," he answered. "We won't know until we have somebody do an audit."

"Whatever the debt," I said confidently, "I believe it's God's will for us to save this ministry. That has to be our goal."

A few days later Jim Thrash the new general manager of WRET (but not of Trinity), paid us a visit. "You owe us $70,000 in production costs," he announced grimly.

I started to tell him we would pay, but he interrupted me. "I don't want to hear what you have to say," he scowled. "I want the money within thirty days or I'm putting you off the air."

"My God will do it," I answered.

And with that, Thrash walked out of the office.

It was impossible to come up with $70,000 in thirty days. We were only drawing $20,000 a month, and we had to pay salaries, equipment costs, building expenses, utilities, and a score of other bills with that.

Give him what he asks, the Lord said, *and I'll do the miracle for you.*

That next Friday, I called Jim Moss into my office, "have one of the girls in bookkeeping make out a check for $20,000 and take it to Jim Thrash this afternoon."

His face flushed, "Jim no way. We don't have it. Our deposits on Monday occasionally reach $7,000 but often less, and that's our big day."

"Write it and take it," I said firmly.

He sat staring incredulously at me. "God told me to do it last night," I said finally.

That afternoon, Moss delivered the $20,000 check to WRET, knowing that amount wasn't in our bank account. For the rest of the day, I noticed him looking pale and sick.

We didn't have time to go on the air and ask our supporters for contributions. Nor was there time to contact them by mail.

Only the Spirit of God could speak to our supporters, and on Monday—it happened!

Thirty thousand dollars came in the mail. It was the greatest miracle of concentrated giving I'd ever witnessed—totally inspired by the Lord. There had been no giving like that before in the ministry.

The following Friday, I felt God speaking to me once again about writing WRET another $20,000 check, and so I told Moss to do it.

"No Jim!" he said, "not again. Please don't ask me to do this. We don't have the money."

"God told me to do it again." I said.

He acquiesced, encouraged, no doubt, by the previous Monday's miracle. Again there was no extra plea for money. We did nothing, but trusted wholly in God, waiting in silence.

But when Monday came, it happened again! Contributions totaling more than $20,000 came in.

Little by little we paid off the overdue bills. But I found new ones every day, stacks of them. As we gradually uncovered the mountain of debts, Moss got on one telephone and I on another, and we called every creditor. "You will be paid within thirty days," I told each creditor. "After that, you will be paid on time, every time, all the time." God honored our pledge.

At first, it looked as if the total indebtedness was in the neighborhood of $150,000, but eventually it amounted to more than $250,000.

The Lord was allowing us to see the debts in just bits and pieces. Jim Moss laughed one day as we neared the end of paying off the debts. "If we'd seen all the debts at one time," he suggested, "I don't believe even Jim Bakker would have had the faith to believe God for it." He was right, but God had not tempted us above that we were able.

With God's mighty help though, we faced every bill individually and paid it as the Holy Spirit directed, no matter what the amount. God never failed us. Our pint-size faith grew larger with every instance.

The Lord knew we would need a larger faith for what lay ahead.

18

The
PTL Club

The image of Trinity Broadcasting Systems had become tarnished as a result of the debts. The ministry needed a change of image—from the one of not paying bills to one of doing everything properly in the sight of God and man.

Using Trinity as the holding company, I decided to call the new corporation the PTL Television Network. And right away, God began blessing our spiritually renewed "PTL Club."

In the meantime, we had begun signing more stations— Columbia, South Carolina, Greenville-Greenwood, Mississippi, Jackson, Tennessee. Eight weeks after we hit the airwaves in Savannah, Georgia, our first telethon was scheduled.

"Savannah is a place heavy with occult spirits," Jim Moss warned in describing Georgia's oldest city. "There is much spiritism and metaphysical activity in town and we'd better be prayed up."

The first two nights of the telethon—Friday and Saturday—were dead. It seemed almost a repeat of our experience in Chattanooga. "But WJCL has a strong signal," I said trying to analyze the situation, "and besides it goes into other cities like Brunswick and Jesup by way of the cable system."

As I prayed God began speaking to my heart. *There is need for forgiveness among the people*, He said. *Under the pressure of work, many brothers and sisters have lost patience with one another. There is need of cleansing and healing. Then, I will hear from heaven and do a work among you such as you have never seen.*

Sunday afternoon, the entire staff met in WJCL's lobby to pray and take communion. People wept. They sang. They praised God. There was rejoicing among everybody as the Spirit of God moved among us through the simple act of receiving communion—partaking of the body and the blood of Jesus.

Sunday night, the bondage was broken. As soon as the telethon resumed, there was an entirely new spirit in the studio. The Envoys, a popular singing group, sang and testified, while accounts of healings, conversions and miracles poured into the station.

"We believe that God will tell forty callers to pledge a thousand dollars each for this ministry in Savannah," I announced in a burst of Spirit-inspired faith. Within thirty minutes those forty persons had made the pledges.

"Folks, please don't give any more," I said later. "We have enough to keep the program on the air in Savannah."

But that didn't stop the pledges. Finally, I walked over to the five rows of phones and began removing the pledge cards from each counselor. "Folks," I pleaded, "we've already reached the goal, and we'd like to keep the lines open for those who call to receive Christ. Please don't call with pledges."

But the calls still came. Almost an hour after we left the air, the twenty-five phones were jammed. The cleansing and communion among the staff members had opened the door for the Holy Spirit to break the occult bondage over the telethon.

With the aid of telethons such as the one in Savannah, our outreach gained momentum. A new spirit of liberty began to radiate from the "PTL Club." The Lord began teaching us the principle of sowing and reaping (Galatians 6:7).

In its infancy, the ministry had purchased a large mobile trailer to use as a temporary office. The idea never worked out and the trailer had sat for many months in the parking lot at WRET.

One day I was driving to the studio when the Lord began speaking to me. *I don't want you to sell that trailer*, He said, *I want you to give it away*. And He told me the name of the person to whom we should give it.

I began to argue, but God quietly reminded me of a verse I had long before memorized. *What about Luke 6:38?* He asked. "Give, and it shall be given unto you; good measure, pressed down, and shaken together, and running over, shall men give into your bosom. For with the same measure that ye mete withal it shall be measured to you again."

That had to work for ministry just as it would for an individual. As soon as I reached the office, I made plans to give the trailer away.

That one decision unleashed a fresh move of God's Spirit among us. Hundreds more began finding Christ every month. The number of confirmed healings increased sizably. And contributions rose dramatically.

In the beginning, PTL operated on such a shoestring budget that guests had to pay their own travel expenses to and from Charlotte to appear on the program. Nor had we ever been financially able to donate to other ministries.

But as God taught us this principle of sowing and reaping, we began to pay our guests' travel expenses and to make contributions to other established groups who sought to proclaim the gospel.

The Cameron family from Scotland was establishing the

159

first Bible school for Spirit-filled believers in their country. They desperately needed financial help, and God told us to give $15,000 to them for the school.

In another instance, we donated an identical amount to Willard Cantelon's radio project in France to help complete their studios. Time after time, we gave and God blessed. But none of the blessings returned as quickly as did the one the day missionary Phil Saint was with us on the "PTL Club."

Phil's brother, Nate had been martyred in 1956 by Auca Indians, a fierce tribe in Ecuador. On the program, Phil was explaining that the group he headed was building a center in Argentina in honor of his brother.

"And we need roughly $2,000 to finish the roof," Phil explained.

As he continued talking, the Lord spoke to me, *Tell him PTL will finish the building*. I thought about all the debts we faced with new equipment purchases. I wanted, foolishly, to tell God I wasn't going to do it. But I bit my tongue and obeyed.

"Phil, we'll give you the $2,000." Tears trickled down his cheeks as he thanked me.

After the show, I went back into my office where the day's current mail awaited me. I opened the top letter. Out fluttered a $2,000 check with a note.

I sat down as tears ran down my face. *Jim, you didn't really give anything away today. I am the source of all things and this is merely a transfer of funds. But you will receive the blessing of giving and of obedience.*

The Lord taught me not only to give financially, but to give of myself to others in need. A.T. Lawing, a charter member of PTL's board and owner of an oil equipment company, came to me one day. "My sales manager has left me, Jim," he said somberly, "and the man's beginning to drain away business from my company. One of my largest customers may go over to him, and, if they do, my business is doomed. I'll go bankrupt after twenty years in business.''

"This is not of God," I answered, trying to encourage A.T. "A child of God should not have this kind of thing happen to him. We're going to do something.''

A.T. still looked worried as he left, but I felt God was moving me to stand with this man who had done so much for others. God spoke to me three times about helping A.T. so a few days later I called the PTL staff together and explained the situation. Then we borrowed a battered red church bus and, with David Kelton driving, we carted some thirty of our employees over to A.T.'s warehouse "to claim the land."

When we arrived A.T. introduced us to all of his people and we all marched into the back of his large warehouse. Using a gas pump still in its carton for a pulpit, we sang hymns and had a regular service. On the basis of Matthew 16:19 and 18:18, we bound the work of the devil and claimed a great victory for God.

Afterwards we laid hands on A.T., his wife and almost every item in the warehouse. A prophecy even came forth that "God would multiply the business . . . and multiply it again.''

Bearing in mind this was 1975, a recession year highlighted by gasoline shortages, God performed a miracle. A.T. sold more gas pumps during the next six months—250 to be exact—than anybody in the entire United States and won the manufacturer's Golden Pump Award.

Throughout the spring and summer months of 1975, a host of new stations were being signed to carry the broadcast. Jim Moss, who had previously operated a cleaning-supply business, was placed in charge of this responsibility. But within a matter of weeks he had produced incredible results. It was as if a seasoned "pro" was handling the task.

"A pro *is* handling it," Moss explained to me one day. "He's the Lord. I know so little about this business that all I do is

161

call people and tell them about PTL. Then the questions come, and I depend entirely on the Holy Spirit to give me wisdom to answer.

"When I told one station owner that we purchased fifty hours each month he was so shocked he literally fell out of his chair. His secretary had to come to the phone while he picked himself up off the floor. Most stations are used to Sunday morning religious programs that can barely pay their bills."

Moss signed up twenty-four stations in a matter of weeks, and when an ABC television owners' meeting in Chicago brought favorable response to our program, another host of stations were signed up nationwide. Station managers in some cities actually told us we outdrew Johnny Carson.

By the end of 1975, we had reached almost every section of the country, having signed a total of forty-six stations.

The work was mushrooming and I needed more staff all the time. Jim Moss as Executive Vice President had become a real gift from God. So had Dale Hill, Sam Orender, Del Holford, David Carver and Roger Wilson in the technical areas. Then, Roger Flessing and Alex Valderrama, who had been with me in California, joined us.

Don Storms, who had been the leader of the Envoys singing group for years, left to come to PTL. Don took over as telethon coordinator and quickly established himself as one of the most valuable people at the network. So had Marian Herbst who took over the bookkeeping department. Marian had worked in city government jobs for years before she joined our staff. She began with us when she volunteered to help me wallpaper the lobby of our Independence Boulevard studios. These people contributed enormously to PTL's rapid success.

One of our crucial needs was for an experienced person to handle the counseling. I knew of only two people qualified for the job: Henry and Susan Harrison, who had worked several years with me on the "700 Club" and the "Jim and Tammy Show."

Working with someone night-after-night, you sometimes develop a close rapport, such as grew between Henry and myself.

Driving back to Charlotte one morning from a telethon in Huntsville, Alabama, I walked into the studios and found Henry Harrison waiting for me.

"Brother," I said, "I don't know if I can take this or not. It's good to see you."

Henry laughed. He was the same good-natured man I had grown to love at CBN.

I shook my head in disbelief. Walking into my office, I attempted to explain. "I was up all last night," I said, "and about 2:30 I cried out to God, 'You've promised me Henry and Susan Harrison for this ministry. I need them!' "

Henry chuckled. "And to walk in and find you here this morning," I continued, "is almost more than I can take."

"Susan and I were awakened about 2:30 and the Lord was telling us to get on the road south. Since we were already on our vacation time, we decided to take off. So we did . . . and here I am."

Air time for the "PTL Club" was nearing as we talked. "Can you be on the program with me today?" I asked.

"Since we're vacationing, I don't see any reason why not," he answered with a grin.

That day Henry appeared on the show and God blessed us wonderfully. Henry's spirit and mine had always been compatible, and that day God's anointing was obvious to everyone.

Afterward, we went out to lunch. "Henry," I said, "I promised God I would never ask you to leave CBN and come with me. But if you ever left for any reason, you'd find PTL's arms open wide to you."

Henry smiled and swallowed hard.

"I'll tell you the truth," I said, "I'm having a hard time staying off my knees in prayer right now."

"I know," Henry answered, "I'd like to come. I feel this is the Lord, but I've got to know for sure. I'll call you."

As Henry left for Atlanta, I felt peace in my heart. I had prayed for him to join us in California, and it had not happened. Now, I believed, was the time for Henry to join PTL.

The next day Henry called. God had spoken to him that now was indeed the time to become part of our team.

Some 10,000 people had received Christ the first year after I returned from the West Coast, but during 1975—once the Spirit of God was free in the ministry—that number doubled. Some of those conversions occurred in the midst of incredible circumstances.

Hazel Williams, one of the ladies in our counseling department, quietly led a fifty-year-old man to the Lord one day. A few hours later that same man was pulled, dead, from beneath his car which had fallen on him as he worked beneath it.

A few weeks later, Hazel had prayed in simple fashion with the distressed wife of a man who was in a coma with terminal cancer at Duke University Medical Center. Within two days, that man was dismissed from the hospital with no trace of cancer anywhere in his body.

Some of the stories are poignant. Karen Smith, one of the ministry's secretaries, began answering phones one day when all the available counselors were occupied. Karen's first caller was a nineteen-year-old girl who had run away from home three years earlier. She was on drugs, pregnant, and living with a man in a town in Tennessee when she flicked on the television one day and began watching the "PTL Club."

With compassion born out of her own struggle to find Christ, Karen comforted the girl. Finding someone who cared and had something real to offer as well, the young girl received Christ into her life. The next day, she left for home to be reunited with her parents.

Twenty-four hours a day, the calls come in. Sickness,

homosexuality, demonism, rebellion, unbelief, financial troubles, marital problems—the list never ends. But as the show is broadcast and people respond, God picks out the right telephone counselor for the person calling. Then the Spirit himself goes to work.

One day over lunch, Jim Moss told me of an incident the previous Saturday night. "I was up in Salisbury speaking at a Full Gospel Businessmen's meeting, and at the end, a woman who looked to be at least eighty years old was wheeled over to me. Her hands were badly palsied, but she clutched my arm tightly, saying, "Jim Moss, I wanted to meet you. You and that Jimmy Bakker are my boys. I watch you every day. You are the one sparkle left in my life."

Tears ran down Jim's face, "And then she reached up with that palsied hand and gave me a yellowed envelope containing three dollars. There wasn't a dry eye in the place."

Tears began to fall from my own eyes. "If PTL did nothing more than brighten up people's days with the hope of Jesus Christ, it would still be all worth it. It would still be all worth it."

19

A Miniature Williamsburg

A month before Henry Harrison and his wife Susan joined our staff to direct the counseling, Ruth and Phil Egert were hired. Phil, who would handle our photography, had been chief photographer at Colonial Williamsburg and photographed Tammy and me back during our early days on the road. His wife, Ruth, who had worked closely with me at CBN, would become my staff assistant.

Noting the large numbers of husbands and wives working for PTL, someone asked, "Why's that?"

"I know that's contrary to the policies of many companies," I answered, "but here we're not out to build a super-corporate structure. This is a team of people who work in harmony and love with one another because they serve Jesus Christ.

"When a husband has to go out of town to work on a telethon, we send his wife with him," I added. "And we've found that it strengthens our work and the marriages."

Interestingly enough, one of the first husband-wife teams we hired was Derek and Dianne Parker. Years before, when I was at CBN, Derek had been that little ten-year-old boy who prayed for his sister with "club feet." Now God had brought us together as He had with many people from our days at CBN and in California.

As I thought of all the people God was bringing together at PTL, I could see that He had new worlds for us to conquer for Jesus. "Devil," I said one day, "you have already lost the battle. This is a united team that God is putting together for the final victory."

We had run out of space at our Independence Boulevard studios. There was no place for the guests to watch the show, and almost no place for our growing staff. I had one secretary working in my office with her desk jammed against mine and another in a cramped space just outside the door.

I was determined not to sink hundreds of thousands of dollars into elaborate and expensive-to-maintain buildings. So, we planned a $60,000 program to purchase and expand into the building next door. Next I offered to buy the service station lot on the corner for parking space.

The property's owner wanted $325,000 at first, but she later came down to a more reasonable $285,000. But, even with this space, we would lack adequate parking very soon after people came to fill the new offices.

In the midst of all the planning, Harvey Watson, our financial consultant, came down from Winston-Salem. He saw the horrible parking situation and quickly realized the filling station lot wouldn't help that much. Taking me aside he said, "Jim, it wouldn't be wise to add to this building. We need to look elsewhere."

I had come to depend on Harvey's sound advice. When we had discovered the enormous debt facing the ministry, it was Harvey who had almost single-handedly rebuilt our accounting system. At another point, he had even saved our non-profit status with the government by locating some legal papers that had been

filed at the wrong location. When Harvey Watson spoke, I had
learned to listen.

"I'm with you, Harvey," I answered. "Why don't you see
what you can find?"

Sometime later Harvey spoke with Margaret Graham, a
local realtor. "If you're looking for property for PTL, I have
something that may be suitable," she suggested.

Harvey was impressed with the building's possibilities and
came looking for me. Collaring Dale Hill and me, we drove over to
an impressive-looking mansion on twenty-five acres of property
off Park Road in southwest Charlotte. It had once been owned by a
wealthy Charlotte contractor.

As we drove up the long driveway, I recognized the value
of the property. "Harvey, don't do this to me," I said laughing.
"I've loved this kind of property ever since I was a kid. But I don't
think we can afford it."

"I don't know about that," Harvey answered, "maybe we
can. Let's look into it anyway."

As we walked through the three-story colonial home with
mahogany-pegged floors and chandeliers, I began to want to
purchase this property for PTL. Later I took the board of
directors—A.T. Lawing, Jim Moss, Bill Flint, Larry Hall—out for
a look, and we voted on the spot to offer the owners $200,000.

At the time, the offer seemed ridiculous. The property's
owners had refused a $550,000 offer earlier.

PTL's offer was to be paid at $25,000 down with monthly
payments of $3,000 to be financed at 7¾ percent by the owners
who would receive, in addition, a $100,000 tax receipt as a bonus
from the ministry.

I had gone to sleep that night when Harvey called on the
phone. They turned our offer down," he announced, a little
dejected.

"I figured they might," I mumbled.

"Guess what they want?" Harvey asked.

"What?"

He laughed. "A $150,000 tax receipt instead of the $100,000 one we originally offered."

"Hallelujah," I shouted. "God's with us in this project."

"The only problem now," Harvey suggested cautiously, "is getting zoning approvals, and that may be a good bit harder since we're going to be in a residential neighborhood."

Harvey was right. The zoning board had trouble rating us. We weren't actually a church. Neither were we a broadcasting station since we didn't have a license from the FCC. But since we did broadcasting work, the board was considering that approach. "We're sorry for the delay in getting you folks rated," a board spokesman told me. "There's never been a group quite like you before."

But as the days passed slowly, I began to fret about the zoning question. The property was occupying much of my time and thoughts; I wanted it too much.

One day after the "PTL Club" had left the air, I was still seated at the set's desk when anxious thoughts of the property began to flood into my mind. "Lord," I prayed, "I'm giving this property over to You. If You don't want us to have it, there are other ways to solve our problems in this building . . . but I'm giving You this property. It's Your business from now on."

I could have kicked myself for having gotten so involved over the property in the first place. Through all the experiences on the West Coast, I should have realized by now that the ministry belonged to the Lord. It was His business to take care of our growing pains, not mine.

In a few days a letter from the planning and zoning board arrived that cleared up the rating dilemma. Now we were free to seek the Lord's guidance with the property.

A few nights later, I had gone home and couldn't sleep. Tammy had already been asleep for an hour or so while I tossed and turned restlessly. I had learned whenever I couldn't sleep to talk to the Lord, or, better, to listen to Him. He was always awake.

"Lord," I questioned, "You've given us this property, what do You want us to do with it?"

Sometime around three o'clock in the morning, the Lord began answering that question.

"I've got it, I've got it," I shouted, forgetting Tammy was asleep beside me.

"What in the world do you mean, 'you've got it?' " she murmured drowsily, "lay down and go to sleep."

But, Tammy, I've got it," I shouted again. "God wants us to build a village, a miniature version of Colonial Williamsburg."

God had imprinted a blueprint of the building in my head. I got out of bed and began drawing it just as I had seen it. With the Carters Grove mansion situated in the front, the buildings would be interconnected with walking paths and flower gardens.

Alex Valderrama took what I had sketched and turned it into something beautiful. It was exactly the picture God had shown me in the vision. We would call it Heritage Village.

Already our staff's dream of a first-class video truck—an idea conceived while we were all "unemployed" in California—had become a reality. Now another dream from that same time, of a first-rate television studio, was taking shape. The studio would be similar in architecture to the Bruton Parish Church at Williamsburg.

The board of directors wholeheartedly endorsed the project, and I began telling our partners and supporters about it over the air. Contributions, love offerings and gifts came from every section of the country.

Supporters in Tennessee sent contributions to furnish one of the mansion's rooms, and we named it in honor of that state. So did the people from Ohio. The increase of income sent our expansion past three thousand percent. "The IBM people say they've never seen any corporation grow this fast," Jeff Rikard remarked one day.

Richard Scarborough, a quiet, soft-spoken man whom God earlier had told me to hire, would oversee the construction. Next, we brought in Laxton Construction Company, Richard's old firm, to do the actual building. Through Laxton, we were able to have Bob Barrier, a Christian, supervise the construction job. Then we found Bob Rash, an architect who liked working with the Williamsburg-style architecture.

October 20, 1975—the day ground was broken for the construction—Mr. Laxton turned to me. "Jim," he said, "we'll take care of the building. You talk to the man upstairs about the weather."

"That's a promise," I answered.

We did and, for over seventy consecutive days, Charlotte, North Carolina, had sunshine right in the middle of its normally rainy winter. The weatherman reported it was the warmest winter on record.

The contractor had estimated it might take as long as six months to get all of the steel for the 54,000-square-foot building on site. But our order arrived two weeks after it was placed.

One day I was standing outside watching the steel being lifted into place. "Some of the construction people say they've never seen steel fit together like this," Barrier reported. "They're not having to make any adjustments. It's uncanny.

"And," he added, "we've had to order brick from Pennsylvania to match the Williamsburg-style of handmade brick we're looking for."

"I didn't know that," I said.

"Yes, and the people in Pennsylvania have promised me the brick next week," he said, "but I don't really believe they'll be able to get it here that fast. It would take a miracle to do that."

I started walking toward my office. As I did, the first truckload of bricks pulled up. "Hey Bob," I shouted, pointing at the truck, "did you say it would take a miracle? Well, there it is!"

20

"I've Planted a Bomb in your Studio!"

Since our lease would be up April 1st on the Independence Boulevard studios, the construction crew began working three shifts a day building the new center. With the aid of a mammoth plastic tent stretched over the top of the steel beams, the crews were able to work even on the days when the weather turned wet.

The first month's payment on the building came to around $100,000, and it was met relatively easily. But then God supplied such beautiful weather, the working hours were increased, and the next month's payment came to $350,000. It seemed impossible for God to supply that amount of money above our normal operating budget, but by the end of the month He had.

Then the Lord turned the rain off completely. January and February's weather became spring-like and the payment rose to $487,000.

When I drove home from the office, I couldn't sleep for thinking about the $487,000. Finally I pulled my jogging clothes on over my pajamas and went outside to run at two o'clock in the morning. A full moon hung in the Carolina sky as I jogged lightly down the street. The night air was refreshing against my face.

"God," I said, "will I ever learn to commit a problem to You and not run back and pick it up?"

The question hung in my mind as I trotted further down the road. Tears dripped down my face wetting the front of my jogging shirt as the anxieties and pressures of the building problems came to the surface.

There was healing and release through the tears, and the next day I confessed to our prayer partners that I had taken more of the burden than I should have. "But," I said tearfully, "I have committed it to God once again, and I'm trusting Him to solve it."

I had fully expected the financial battle to be our toughest obstacle to the building program—especially since the Lord had instructed me to pay cash as I went.

But soon we encountered new and different roadblocks.

Rigorous safety standards began to be enforced by the city inspectors. "I've never seen a job with these kind of standards being enforced," Richard Scarborough reported. "It's almost as if somebody is trying to close down the construction."

That thought hadn't entered my mind, even though I realized the center was being built in an influential residential area of Charlotte. But then came a more serious problem.

"I've just gotten a call," Scarborough said late one Friday afternoon, "that unless we meet with the building inspectors on Monday the city will close down the project. They've already told some people at Laxton to be at the meeting."

"What's the problem?" I asked perplexed. "Aren't we meeting the building code standards?"

"Sure we are," he answered nodding his head. "I'm not sure what they want, but I'll find out Monday."

"There's nothing to it," Scarborough reported after getting back from the meeting. "We just had to go over some changes in our blueprints with the city."

I quickly breathed a sigh of relief, thinking we had cleared another giant hurdle. But my relief was only short-lived. Wild rumors began filtering to me that we had plans to put up a building as tall as the NCNB building in downtown Charlotte. Another rumor speculated that over 100,000 people would be attending our planned July 4th dedication ceremony.

The rumors were completely satanic. Newspaper articles—one headline read, "PTL Saving Souls and Raising Dollars"—helped fan the unfounded rumors.

Next came a printed announcement that the neighborhood association would meet to discuss the impact of our construction in the area. "If you have no concern for the investment you have in your home or the safety of your children, read no further and throw this announcement in the wastebasket," the sheet proclaimed.

"I think we ought to go to that meeting," I told Jim Moss. "In fact, I think we should take some of our employees so they can know about this situation and stand with us. Perhaps we can temper the meeting some."

Moss shook his head. "I doubt that very much. From the tenor of this sheet, these people are angry and they're likely to try to close our building project down."

"That may be true, but at least they ought to let me present our side of the picture."

I was mistaken. Three hundred gathered in a nearby elementary school for the meeting. Their emotions were running so high that night I had no opportunity to present our plans. The association's members presented a one-sided view of the whole situation.

"They're going to put fourteen more buildings on that property," one man said angrily.

"I've heard they will erect a building taller than any in Charlotte," another said.

A gray-headed woman stood. "This is going to wreck our neighborhood," she said tearfully. "It won't be a decent place to live!"

175

And with that the list of complaints grew:
—traffic congestion and hazards
—safety of children
—noise and air pollution
—declining property values
—high-rise buildings going up

The crowd's disposition became nastier. One man tried to speak. People thought he was PTL's lawyer. "Sit down and shut up," the crowd roared, "we told you, you couldn't talk."

Finally, Jim Atkins, PTL's attorney, stood up and identified himself. Only then did the crowd relent and allow the other man to speak.

Another man stood. "PTL was supposed to leave a buffer zone of two hundred feet between their buildings and other residential property. We've looked at their plans, and they've violated that specification."

Realizing the error of what the man had said, I identified myself and asked to explain the situation.

"Boo-oo-oo-oo! Hiss-ss-ss-ss! Sit down! Shut up! We don't want anything out of you!"

I was stunned. Momentarily, I looked down at Tammy who was crying. Her body twitched nervously.

Finally, someone spoke up. "He's a homeowner," they shouted, "a member of the association. He has a right to speak."

"Folks," I said, addressing the crowd with the friendliest tones I could muster, "the construction referred to within the two hundred foot buffer zone is a driveway that was originally put into the property over twenty years ago."

"Humph," the crowd was slightly mollified.

"But I would like to add this," I said. "If you want us out of the neighborhood, we don't want to be here. The PTL Heritage Village is for sale for exactly what we have invested in it. You can buy it if you want it. People—Christians—all over America have contributed their money for its construction. We'll sell it if we have to, but we won't give it away!"

And with that I sat down. The meeting continued with people apparently turning a deaf ear to my comments. Doug Bell, a local broadcaster, stood and asked "for two minutes of silent prayer" to help settle the air.

But that still didn't calm people's ruffled emotions. As the meeting closed, a collection was taken for legal fees "to see what we can do about stopping the PTL construction project."

Many of our younger staff members had never faced an emotionally-charged situation like this before. "Let's go back to the mansion for a prayer meeting," I suggested. The neighborhood people's reaction to our construction project had unnerved us all.

"We've been through this kind of thing before," I explained back at the mansion, "and God has seen us through each time. Stay prayerful. We have nothing to fear. Jesus is still on the throne."

As all seventy-five of us knelt and prayed for God's intervention, a prophecy came forth in tongues. Jim Atkins, our lawyer, interpreted: *The battle is Mine saith God. As I have spoken to My servants from the dawn of creation, lean not on your worldly devices, but lean on Me. Trust in Me. Then watch My mighty arm deliver you from the snare. Remember the battle is Mine. The victory is won. Keep yourselves joyful in Me. My joy is your strength.*

I was deeply troubled by the obstacles facing us, but each time I began to grow weary, God would bring forth another message of encouragement.

The very next day on the set during the program, for example, Bob Bartlett, founder-director of Teen Challenge in Philadelphia, prophesied, *No hand that is against My work shall be allowed to stand.* Almost simultaneously, an identical prophecy was spoken at the mansion where another prayer meeting was being conducted.

The following day, Don Hughes, an evangelist from Oklahoma, spoke another prophecy. *I have chosen you from among many to lead My work. I am with you. This problem is only for a short season. Trust Me.*

That's what I was trying to do. Trust God—yet the difficulty persisted. Tammy Sue and her cousin, Jesse, were playing in our backyard when rocks were thrown at them. Next, a suspicious phone call came asking where Tammy Sue was. The caller wouldn't identify himself and hung up quickly.

Rumors continued to fly. One man was reported to have said he would bomb or burn the PTL center.

Finally in desperation, I wrote a letter to the neighborhood association sending it by registered mail. "We have done everything within our power to cooperate with you," I wrote, ". . . we have been willing to discuss problems with anyone at anytime . . . but the anger and heat that has been stirred up has caused more damage than PTL could have ever inflicted upon this neighborhood.

"I am holding you, the board of directors and leaders, responsible for allowing such vicious rumors and statements of hate to be spread, without one of you speaking up and speaking out for unity, harmony, and discussion in this matter. I beg of you, let us come together and solve these problems before they get out of hand any more than they already are."

One evening about eight o'clock, our twenty-four hour counseling center received a call. "Hello, praise the Lord," the counselor said. "May I help you?"

"There's a bomb planted in your studio," a muffled voice announced.

"What did you say?" the counselor asked.

"I've planted a bomb in your studio," came the hurried reply and then the line went dead.

Two blue and white Charlotte police cars screeched to a halt shortly after they were notified of the bomb threat. Hurriedly the four policemen ushered everybody out of the Independence Boulevard building, and began to search the offices and studios.

Thirty minutes later Richard Scarborough phoned me at home. "There's been a bomb threat," he said excitedly, "the police are on their way to the Heritage Center to check it out. I'll be there in a few minutes."

"Oh, no," Tammy replied when I told her.

Overhearing the conversation Tammy Sue spoke up. "Daddy, they're not going to bomb our pretty studios, are they?" she asked. "It's okay to bomb the old studios, but not the new ones."

Henry Harrison and Richard Scarborough arrived shortly, and we drove the few hundred yards from my house to the studio. The sprinklers were on, sending water splattering around the grounds and brick sidewalks.

We rang the doorbell, trying to find Mary Jo and Elwin Hendrickson, grounds keepers who lived in the mansion. "Surely, they're somewhere around," I said nervously, "since the sprinklers are on."

Except for the sound of the sprinklers, the Heritage Center was quiet as a tomb. Finally several policemen drove up and, with flashlights in hand, they roamed the area looking for what might look like a bomb.

Since we couldn't locate any of the staff, wild thoughts kept plaguing my mind . . . "maybe the staff members have been tied up and left in a back room . . . what if they're dead?"

I didn't know if the steeple atop the Bruton Parish building would suddenly be set in orbit or not. "You'd better not hang around the buildings right now, Reverend Bakker," one of the policemen suggested. "We've searched the place thoroughly, but in all the maze of construction, a bomb could have been planted anywhere.'"

Then the Hendricksons walked up. They had been out shopping for shrubbery. My fears were allayed.

My face was damp from the night air. "God," I said looking up at the steeple, "have we come this far with this building to have the whole thing exploded by a bomb?"

Henry and Richard had already left when I began walking back home. I wondered if the center would ever be finished. It was a dark night, almost as dark as the night I had left CBN when I stepped out into that sheet of blackness. Tammy and I went to sleep that night not knowing whether we'd be awakened by an explosion or not.

"We're going to have to cancel our big plans for the Fourth of July celebration," Jim Moss said walking into my office the next day.

"I know," I answered. "I've been sitting here thinking about that. We need to do everything we can to preserve peace, so we might as well announce it now."

"Okay," he agreed, "I'll contact the papers about the change, and then we can notify Bob Harrington about the rally being canceled."

Moss left and I mentally ran over all the things that had occurred in the last several days: rumors, bomb threats, insults, name calling, lawyers hired, suits threatened. Where would it all end?

"Lord," I prayed. "You gave us this property, and I can't believe You will allow it to be taken away now. God, You made us a promise, and I believe heaven and earth will pass away before You break a promise."

Unless God intervened, it seemed, with the neighborhood association's political clout in Charlotte, we were doomed. The building might be a hollow skeleton standing vacant for months. The PTL Heritage Center would never be used unless God performed a miracle. Our backs were to the wall as never before.

21

"An Oasis among tall Trees"

Someone had suggested that both sides' lawyers needed to meet and talk. An almost certain lawsuit was in the wind. That following Saturday afternoon, in the plush quiet of law offices high above downtown Charlotte, the attorneys met.

The neighborhood association asked for many things I considered a hindrance to the ministry. But the meeting ended peacefully and cordially. Going into the session, God had reminded me that blessed are the peacemakers, and I carried that Scripture within me throughout the day.

It looked as if a reasonable solution might be worked out for both sides. There was a ray of hope.

That afternoon Tammy heard the doorbell ringing. "I'm Mrs. McBride," the young woman said handing Tammy a freshly-baked cake. "I'm one of your neighbors." Tammy invited her in and they chatted briefly.

"I just wanted you to know," said Mrs. McBride, "there has been a prayer meeting going on in this neighborhood for years.

181

Last year, a minister-friend of ours was traveling from New York to Florida and stopped off here. During a prayer meeting, he prophesied that the neighborhood would open up for the Lord. He said it would become an oasis among tall trees.''

"Praise the Lord," Tammy exclaimed. "Since the new center has one of the largest pecan trees in North Carolina and several other giant walnut trees, the prophecy fits us. Doesn't it?"

Mrs. McBride smiled. "Sounds like it," she answered. "What's interesting is that the prophecy was spoken months before you folks bought the Heritage property."

Tammy called me at the office to tell me about Mrs. McBride's visit, and I shared the prophecy with Jim Moss and members of our staff. Everyone tearfully got on their knees and thanked God.

The staff meeting broke up and I walked back alone to the new studio building. It had rained that afternoon. The air was clean. The orange sun was sliding into the westward sky. It seemed like a million tons had lifted off me as I walked around the center's grounds looking at the buildings . . . reveling in the floral gardens . . . and the lushness of the trees.

For so many weeks I had been wondering whether we would ever be able to use the buildings we had worked so hard to build. God had already produced over one million dollars in cash payments for the structures. I longed to get my thoughts and energies back to broadcasting—away from the turmoil of construction projects and struggling with people vowing to close us down at any moment.

The ministry was growing so fast. Income had increased from five million to twenty million in one year, and was expected to top a hundred million the next year. Offers and affiliate signings were coming daily from many sources. One offer came to put the "PTL Club" on worldwide satellite. We would be able to minister to every nation in the world.

"An Oasis among tall Trees"

I had always believed that Christian television would be the tool to usher in the triumphant return of the Lord Jesus Christ. And with satellite communications, who knows?

God's presence seemed to descend on the center's property as the sun inched slowly down. It was quiet, peaceful. I hadn't felt this way in a long time. The rain had been a cleansing, almost as if God had cleared the air.

I had hope. A strong wave of hope just seemed to bathe me. I knew then we would occupy the new studios in spite of the threats and bomb scares. We would go forward until Jesus comes.

Inquiries should be addressed to

The PTL Club
Box 15000
Charlotte, North Carolina 28210